From the acclaimed creator of *Snuggle Bunny Book Club*™

Untamed Chaos

A Parent's Guide to Improving Communication, Resolving Conflict, and Restoring Peace in Your Home

Dr. Teri Rouse

Educator, Early & Behavior Interventionist, Autism & Reading Specialist

Untamed Chaos
A Parent's Guide to Improving Communication,
Resolving Conflict, and Restoring Peace in Your Home

drterirouse.com

Copyright © 2024 Dr. Teri Rouse

All rights reserved
No portion of this book may be reproduced mechanically, electronically, or by any other means, including photocopying, without securing the advanced written permission of the author, except in the case of the worksheets, which are meant for individual/family use only. Likewise, no portion of this book may be posted to a website or distributed by any other means without securing the advanced written permission of the author.

Limits of liability and disclaimer of warranty
This book is strictly for informational and educational purposes only. Neither the author nor the publisher shall be liable for any misuse of the enclosed material. The author and the publisher do not guarantee that anyone following these techniques, suggestions, tips, ideas, or strategies will be successful or healed. The author and the publisher shall have neither liability nor responsibility to anyone with respect to any loss or damage caused, or alleged to be caused, directly or indirectly, by the information or suggestions contained in this book.

Medical disclaimer
To the extent that any medical or health information is shared in this book, it is provided as an information resource only and is not to be used or relied on for any diagnostic or treatment purposes. Any such information does not constitute patient information, does not create any patient-physician relationship, and should not be used as a substitute for professional diagnosis and treatment.

Published by Made to Change the World™ Publishing
Nashville, Tennessee

Cover and interior design by Chelsea Jewell

ISBN: 978-1-956837-28-5 Hardback
        978-1-956837-29-2 eBook

Printed in the USA, Canada, Australia, and Europe

To the parents living in chaos who have tried all the traditional methods without success and are still asking, yearning, and pleading for help.

Help is here.

You are not alone.

I see you.

I hear you.

I am you.

This book is dedicated to you—from one parent to another.

Contents

Foreword	ix
Acknowledgments	xv
Introduction	xix

1 The REAL in REAL Peaceful Parenting — 01
    Overview of REAL — 01
    Special Note — 03
    REAL Important Takeaways — 03
    Working Journal Activity 1 — 08

2 The Power of Words and Positive Attention — 13
    The Power of Words — 13
    The BARC System — 14
    Positive Attention — 14
    REAL Important Takeaways — 19
    Working Journal Activity 2 — 22

3 With Big Choices and Decisions Come BIG Emotions — 23
    Why Are Big Emotions BIG? — 28
    A Starting Strategy to Build Decision-Making Muscles — 30
    REAL Important Takeaways — 30
    Working Journal Activity 3 — 33

4 The Good, the Bad, the Reality: Understanding and Accepting Consequences — 35
    What Are Consequences? — 36
    Learning About Consequences — 36
    The Good, the Bad, the Reality — 37
    REAL Important Takeaways — 40
    Working Journal Activity 4 — 42

5 Strike a Pose: React or Respond — 43
- Reacting and Responding — 44
- To Respond or React, That Is the Question — 45
- What You Say — 46
- What You Do — 47
- REAL Important Takeaways — 49
- Working Journal Activity 5 — 52

6 Routine Versus Flexible Schedule — 53
- Creating a Flexible Schedule/Routine — 54
- Homework, the Bane of a Parent's Existence — 59
- REAL Important Takeaways — 62
- Working Journal Activity 6 — 64

7 What to Expect With Expectations — 67
- Expectations for the Entire Family — 68
- Expectations for You and Your Spouse — 70
- Creating Expectations and Consequences — 71
- REAL Important Takeaways — 73
- Working Journal Activity 7 — 75

8 Surround Yourself With Boundaries — 77
- Positive Peeps — 79
- Negative Nellies — 80
- Define Your Boundaries — 82
- REAL Important Takeaways — 83
- Working Journal Activity 8 — 85

9 Self-Care Is Not Selfish! — 87
- Me, Myself, and I Care — 89
- Keeping the Honeymoon Alive — 90
- Your Monkeys, Your Circus — 91
- REAL Important Takeaways — 92
- Working Journal Activity 9 — 94

10 Pearls and Diamonds	97
A Note from Me to You	99
About the Author	101
Testimonials	103
Snuggle Bunny Book Club™	106
Lily's Hope Foundation	107
Resources	109

Foreword

"I *must* put you on bedrest immediately. No question, you have to stop working."

"Your baby will be born early, and it may not make it."

"Your baby could have lifelong complications."

These statements, spoken to me by physicians days before I gave birth and many days after my daughter was born, were my and my husband, Justin's, introduction to parenthood. Lilian Hope was born seven weeks early with many complications. She was small for her gestational age due to a placental abruption and preeclampsia. At two pounds, twelve ounces, our baby girl came into the world with commanding force but was critically ill. Her lungs weren't fully developed, so she needed to be on a ventilator and an oscillator. She had a brain bleed and different-sized kidneys and needed a chest tube, a feeding tube, and so much more.

When we looked at this tiny, fragile fifteen-inch baby in her isolette, swimming in a sea of tubes and wires, we were overwhelmed as new parents. When a nurse in the NICU asked me if I wanted to change Lily's diaper for the first time, my immediate response was, "No, I'll watch you do it first." Our emotions were in a state of chaos … we had no skills, no tools to manage ourselves. Self-care went out the window. We forgot to eat, and sleep was a novelty. We had so many questions:

- Will she make it?
- What would happen to her?
- Could we care for her?
- What do we need to do to care for her?
- How many more days until we can hold her?

People had lots to say about what we should do and how we should do it. Some folks were helpful, but many people just wanted to give their opinions even when they had *no* idea what we were experiencing. So many opinions … so many overstepped boundaries.

Although Lily's NICU stay was traumatic for all of us, her story has a happy ending. After twenty-four days, she came home at three pounds, eleven ounces. And although we were still struggling emotionally, we adjusted. Home life was chaotic, but Lily blossomed. She had walking and talking delays, but, with the help of early intervention services for speech therapy, physical therapy, and occupational therapy, she walked at twenty-one months and started talking at twenty-four months. Lily struggled with a variety of health issues, and, eventually, had surgery at age five to combat them. We'd made it. We were beginning to see the light at the end of the tunnel and considered having another child.

We truly wanted to have a big family, and after much reflection, research, reading, and prayer, we decided to move forward. I quickly got pregnant. And then I had a miscarriage. Let the chaos continue. Tears, guilt, and gut-wrenching sadness came over me. I was in disbelief and suffered more crossed boundaries, lack of self-care, and questions, questions, questions.

A few months before Lily's sixth birthday, I found out I was pregnant again. However, our joy turned to fear as my blood pressure rose, and I was quickly put on medication and bedrest. Even with all of these interventions, I felt, in my gut, that Aiden's delivery would be like Lily's. It was. Again, our world was spinning, and the chaos returned. Aidan came into the world with the same force that Lily did, but his blood pressure crashed, and initially, he was not responsive. Thanks to the medical team, Aidan came around.

We were back in the NICU with a four-pound, eleven-ounce baby. The sights, sounds, and chaos felt familiar. And this time, I was comfortable in the chaos.

Lily anxiously waited to meet her new brother while both Justin and I remained at Aidan's bedside. Thankfully, his NICU stay wasn't as long as Lily's, and we could head home sooner to start our new life as a family of four.

Over the long term, Aidan had gastrointestinal and pulmonary issues like Lily, as well as severe allergies and asthma due to his prematurity. We saw specialists, and, like Lily, he also went through early intervention for physical and speech therapy.

Lily and Aidan both had very rough beginnings. But with their will and strength, along with their wonderful doctors, and a lot of hope and prayers, they were able to rise above it all.

After the chaos of Lily's and Aiden's births, we felt compelled to help other families like ours. Premature births are difficult to anticipate, and many families don't have the time or resources to prepare for their child's early arrival. Premature babies have special requirements, like specific car seats for infants under five pounds, special clothing with buttons and Velcro for cords and IVs, and much more. These additional needs can be very expensive and hard to find in a short amount of time. We wanted to help families navigate the initial struggles of living between home and hospital by providing gift cards for gas, meals, and groceries. And we wanted to provide a welcome home package with items necessary to start off at home safely and comfortably. Based on our journey, and to help families who shared our experience, we established the Lily's Hope Foundation to provide resources for premature babies and their families. Although we started supporting families long before, we got our official 501(c)(3) designation in 2013 and had our big kickoff in 2014.

Our extended family and friends became vital to the growth of Lily's Hope. In 2016, my dad dedicated all his time to supporting the foundation. Justin and I worked full time during the weekdays, and on nights and weekends, we spent our free time with the kids or pouring our time into Lily's Hope … with the kids. Lily's Hope grew so quickly that we had to move the foundation (particularly the donated inventory) to its own space.

Shortly before we moved into our first official office, my dad had a massive and debilitating stroke. He almost didn't survive. Chaos, fear, frustration … again.

- How could this happen?
- What would happen to him?
- What did we need to do to care for him?

All the same questions from Lily's and Aiden's births came flooding back. My dad was our right-hand man. Not only did he dedicate forty hours a week to Lily's Hope, he also was our babysitter and helped with after-school bus pickups and sports practices, all while taking care of my ailing mother. After the stroke, he was nonverbal, and his right side was paralyzed. He had to move into inpatient rehab. One month after my dad's stroke, my mom had a stroke as well. Without my dad to care for her, we had to move my mom to a facility permanently. Two kids, two parents in different facilities needing all kinds of care. Fortunately, though things were chaotic, we were able to work through a lot of the struggles and attend to our self-care. We had help and support, and we continued doing what we do!

After five months of inpatient rehab, my dad came to live with us. That was a new kind of chaos! I had no idea the emotional and physical toll his care would take on all of us. Aides were in our home caring for him over sixty hours per week. I needed to accompany him to frequent doctor's appointments and manage his medication, therapies, and so much more. The minute I walked in from work, I became his aide until the next morning, physically transferring him into bed. Somehow, I still parented an eleven-year-old and a five-year-old through sports and school activities; ran Lily's Hope Foundation; and worked my regular job. *Chaos.* The time my dad lived with us was some of the best and toughest, and I have every confidence we added years onto his life and life into those years. But, ultimately, he needed the care only available in a facility: readily available medical personnel, laundry service, and social events. Yet people questioned our decisions.

Over the next years, we sold our home, changed jobs, and grappled with health issues, surgeries, and the passing of some of our closest relatives. These moments were chaotic but beautiful. They were full of milestones, achievements, and truly amazing times. And we were able to step back and see our own growth and our ability to accept and be present in every situation.

Lily and Aidan are thriving … growing up! They are successful student scholars and athletes! They continue to contribute to Lily's Hope, which is succeeding as an all-volunteer organization!

Since we started, we have supported over five thousand families across the United States, and we have eighteen hospital partners. We have written a few books, expanded the office, opened a subchapter, and so much more. If we didn't have love and support, none of this would have been possible. But we also had to learn to navigate the challenges that were presented along the way. Learning to be flexible and adaptive to change helped us be more present while living in these untamed, chaotic times.

Dr. Teri has been in our world since Lily was about two years old. We met at Chestnut Hill College, where Dr. Teri taught and worked with my aunt, Sister Marie. They put together an event to support Lily's Hope called Lily's Loop, where the entire school and surrounding communities were invited to walk a loop around the campus. It included a bake sale, raffle tickets, games, and all kinds of donated food. While this may seem like a small thing, the impact was huge. People from all over made donations. And many later sought us out to help their family and friends who were in need. The circle just continued to get bigger … and better!

While sometimes I wish that I'd had a guardian angel to help us through those chaotic and challenging times, I realize now that I have that guidance to offer others. I love being a part of Dr. Teri's book to model these fundamental tips and reinforce the wisdom that she shares. Her support has helped us to get through many previous challenges and will continue through any chaos that might still come our way.

This is life … unpredictable. But you can live for today. See and appreciate the beauty around you, and use the multitude of tools offered to learn and grow. Wherever you are on life's journey, I hope you can look through the chaos to find hope, love, and joy, and truly live for the moment.

Jenn Driscoll
Founder, Lily's Hope Foundation

Acknowledgments

There are so many people who have influenced my path in life. I would be remiss if I didn't acknowledge them as a huge part of this journey.

My mom and dad: for knowingly and unknowingly modeling courage, honesty, flexibility, persistence, and determination and being the best parents you knew how to be (which were pretty damn awesome!).

Kristen: first, for making me a parent; second, for inspiring me to always be a better person; and third, for being the motivation to move forward when I didn't think I could!

My husband, Dr. Fred: for supporting me as a parent and stepparent; for believing I was smart enough when I didn't believe that I was; for encouraging me to return to school; for understanding my intensity throughout my teaching experiences; and for constantly supporting me to follow my big hairy-scary dreams.

Dr. Carol Pate, Dr. Jessica Kahn, Dr. Theresa Carfagno, and the Sisters of St. Joseph, especially Sister Marie Bambrick, Sister James Agnes, and Sister Dorothy B.: for being my greatest Griffin cheerleaders as I navigated the doctoral process and now for becoming my lifelong friends and supporters of my mission.

Dr. Jenny Cressman, the best educator on the planet: for encouraging me, with egg on my face, to pursue my doctorate; for co-teaching with me; for sharing my mission of family first; and for sharing your love of children's literature with everyone you meet.

School of Education, Arcadia University: for teaching me how to write; for giving me the tools to be a better teacher and parent; and for the positive behavior foundation that helped me to create the tips, tools, and techniques in this book.

Deana Ramsey and the John L. Kinsey School faculty, staff, and students: for the opportunity to implement tips, tools, and techniques based on positive behavior in your school and classrooms. We made many positive changes in the school culture.

My Sedona Sisters … I hear you … I see you … I am with you.

Justin, Jennifer, Lily, and Aiden Driscoll and Lily's Hope Foundation: for the opportunity to be a part of the greater good for families with preemies.

Division of International Special Education and Services: for giving me the opportunity to broaden my knowledge and to travel the world so I could share with my students and their families.

All of my former students around the world: for teaching me even more than I taught you! I wouldn't be who I am today without each one of you.

Dr. Jonathan Moselle: for talking me off the ledge countless times and encouraging me to write a book using my education and expertise for families … just like yours … and mine.

Jack Canfield and Patty Aubery: for helping me to see my value and purpose and helping me share it with the world.

Lisa Nichols: for pulling me on stage and calling me out so I could discover the clarity to not only write this book but to step into my power to empower.

Sean Smith: for sharing your inspiring personal journey and

heartfelt book, *Daddy, Are You Proud of Me?* It is a masterpiece that all parents and children should read and experience.

Dolly Parton: for our shared passion to get free books, stories, and good literature to families of all income levels.

LeVar Burton and Fred Rogers: for your fantastically family-centered TV shows that inspired children to reach for the moon and grab the stars along the way.

Michelle and Barack Obama: for demonstrating strength and grace in the most challenging situations.

Bob Delaney: for bringing PTS(S) to the attention of the world by sharing your research and personal experiences.

Jane Goodall: for all things humane. Thank you for sharing your bright light with our world.

And Ellie: for believing in my mission and creating a clear pathway so that I would believe too. Thank you for your love, support, critique, and wisdom. This would not have been possible without you. Love you … mean it.

Introduction

> "It's your outlook on life that counts. If you take yourself lightly and don't take yourself too seriously, pretty soon you can find the humor in our everyday lives. And sometimes it can be a lifesaver."
> —Betty White

8:03 am. The phone blared, and the caller ID showed 1-800-PRINCIPAL. I couldn't believe it! Our son, Matthew, hadn't even been in school for an hour, and already, the principal was calling. It was the third time just that week that we had gotten a phone call from his school. I couldn't even imagine what he had done this time.

With sweaty palms and my heart in my throat, I picked up the phone. The principal didn't say good morning; he didn't even call me by name; he simply screamed, "Do you want to know what your son has done this time? He stole a scale from the chemistry lab! And he disconnected the entire computer network in the high school!" Panic, anger, frustration, and disappointment set in. The principal demanded I come and get my son immediately. "In fact, I want both you and his father here to pick him up."

At the time, I was a classroom teacher. I hadn't even finished my morning coffee, and I had to get to work. My husband had clients that he needed to attend to. For the third time that week, we put everything on hold to deal with the crisis that was becoming our family norm.

When we arrived at the school, Mr. Principal told us that our son was going to be suspended for five days. I remember thinking, "What good is that going to do? How is this a solution to the problem?" He would be at home playing video games all day. Exactly where he wanted to be. Not only was that day going to be disrupted, the next five school days would be too. And possibly the rest of his schooling years. I knew that we couldn't carry on like this. My husband couldn't take it anymore; our daughter couldn't take it anymore; and, ultimately, our son couldn't take it anymore.

The suspension led to Matthew's placement in an alternative school. This "special school" had faculty and staff who specialized in helping children who exhibited challenging behaviors, like our son. Though we asked for help and support and followed through with the suggestions they made as best as we knew how, his behavior continued to escalate, and his high school career ended with him dropping out three months before graduation.

At that point, we didn't have too much say in what he decided to do. He wanted to be as far away from us as possible. He thought if he could be free of us, he would be able to do whatever he wanted. He moved in with relatives who enabled his "bad behavior," and he continued to get into trouble. There were no consequences when he stole from other family members. They chalked it up to Matthew needing whatever he stole. There were no repercussions for smoking or using jimmy-rigged black lights to grow marijuana in a closet. Over time, there was little to no contact. We only knew some of what was going on through family, who, nevertheless, continued to belittle us. The chaos lingered … on and on.

Despite Matthew moving out, pain, frustration, fear, and anger remained … trauma. And though we sought help to navigate through these feelings and emotions, we continued to be the butt of jokes and snarky comments from family and friends. We were "those parents"—the ones who entered a room to halted conversations and whispers. The ones that set the rumor mill turning. The ones who couldn't control their son's behavior.

We felt like we had failed as parents and as a family. We felt alone, scared, and angry. We had tried all of the traditional methods: counseling, family and individual therapy, medication. We yelled, cried, and begged. Nothing worked for us. We had looked for help everywhere we could think of and couldn't find it. Some of our family told us we were doing everything wrong. Our friends shunned us. At a time when we most needed connection, all we found was isolation and shame.

I discovered in my search for help, however, that there were parents out there just like us—parents who were fighting similar battles and also looking for help. We weren't alone. We hadn't failed our son or ourselves. We just didn't have the tools to successfully navigate through the chaos. I often wondered if we had started earlier, would we have been able to address the issues when our son was younger? What if we had different ways to respond to the challenges? What if we knew how to communicate better? After our son left, I tapped into resilience I didn't even know I possessed. I began to feel empowered to do better and to not give up on my family. Ultimately, through a chain of events that included going back to school, I was able to change our outlooks and attitudes and improve the quality of our lives in our home.

Unfortunately, I didn't get the knowledge, tools, and skills until it was too late to repair the relationship with Matthew. To this day, he remains separated from us. But our daughter, my husband, and I are in a really good place. We have navigated through the chaos and come out on the other side! The experience with Matthew was a tremendously motivating factor because I hated how we felt and how we were treated. I wanted others to know that there was someone who would listen and who could help them work through similar situations.

After all of the experiences I had in my own family and in the classrooms where I taught, I've made it my life's purpose, through early intervention, to ensure that other families don't have to feel the way we did. I want them to find the help they need even on the frontlines of the chaos. I want to help families cultivate the resilience to weather the storms and become empowered to make best choices and decisions; to help children build autonomy and have the chance to recognize their greatness; and, finally, to improve the quality of family life through better communication and conflict-resolution.

If you've gotten this far in this book, you probably identify with my story and have been looking for answers for a long time. You know that the stakes for not doing something different are just too high. Your time is now. The sooner you make sense of the chaos you are living in, the sooner you can create the peaceful life that you and your family want and deserve!

Early intervention really works! And you don't have to do it yourself. You shouldn't. It's okay to ask for help; in fact, it's a skill set that you'll want to model and teach to your children so that they know how to appropriately ask for help when they need it. Being human can be messy. We all have chaos in one form or another, but we don't have to accept that chaos reigns. Having the right tools will assist you with finding your way back to sanity. That is what this book is about.

My name is Dr. Teri Rouse. I'm a behavior and early interventionist, reading and autism specialist, positive behavior support facilitator, multiple best-selling author, and an educational coach and consultant for parents who are looking for ways to create the peaceful life they want with and for their children. As you turn the pages of this book, you are making a decision to not stay stuck in chaos. To find peace in your home ... quickly. To better communicate with your children and resolve conflicts with less stress and more calm, which is key!

I have been where you are. I know what those sleepless nights feel like. I know that, right now, you are losing touch with your partner and with yourself while trying to keep a smile on your face so the people around you don't know how difficult it all really is. I know you don't believe you're good enough, and I know you don't have the capacity to add one more thing to your to-do list. That's why this book and its advice will meet you right where you are and help you with immediate impact and results. You don't have years to figure this out. The lives of the people you love are on the line. It is never too late to change the course you and your family are on. There is hope! It's not easy, but I promise you that it's worth it. And so are you. Remember … I see you, I hear you, I am you! And there is a way out.

To assist in your journey from chaos into a life of peace and tranquility, I have included a resource page at untamedchaosbook.com/resources that you can consult as you go through this book. The Working Journal on that page includes activities that correlate to each chapter. It is also there for your convenience so that you can take notes, draw pictures, doodle, or write down your thoughts or questions.

The resource page also includes all kinds of helpful hints, suggestions, hands-on material, and downloadables. Go ahead and check them out. And let's get started!

CHAPTER 1

The REAL in REAL Peaceful Parenting

*"Start where you are.
Use what you have.
Do what you can."*
—Arthur Ashe

Overview of REAL

You're getting "those" phone calls; your children are screaming; your friends are avoiding you; your extended family has snarky stuff to say. How do you go from this chaotic noise to a place where you can think clearly, feel kindly, want to be in the same blessed room as your children … to peace and tranquility? Enter REAL Peaceful Parenting.

The four philosophies of REAL—resilience, empowerment, autonomy, and quality of life—together become the fundamentals that build strong people, and strong people build strong families.

These four philosophies are the foundation of moving through the muck and into the light; of finding the strength, independence, love, and peace you crave to create in your home; of finding your own very special and individual greatness.

Let's face it, there is and always will be chaos. And while it can't be avoided, it can be mastered. You already have what you need inside you. These four fundamentals are the muscles that grow with every challenge, every argument, every phone call. Now is the time to use them to create the life you want for you and your children!

R = Resilience

Having resilience and being resilient means that you can gather your inner strength. This inner strength helps you respond to the challenges that you face in a way that keeps you calm and in control. It also allows you to bounce back from those challenges without being overwhelmed and overcome by them. Resilience helps you communicate more clearly and calmly. It helps to build a sense of empathy and understanding that enables families to connect and develop strong bonds. This is critical because by building strong positive relationships with family and friends, you have support and can be accepted during the good and bad times.

E = Empowerment

Empowerment means having power and control over your thoughts, choices, and life. It means having the knowledge of what your options are and getting the support that is right for you. Empowerment means that people are equals. All are respected and confident in your circle. Empowering your children is an important part of effective parenting. You help your children by giving them the tools and skills they need to become confident, independent, and resilient human beings. As parents, you want to help your children grow a strong sense of self-worth and self-esteem, which, ideally, will lead them to a happy and successful life.

A = Autonomy

By its simplest definition, autonomy is a person's ability to act on his or her own. It is a skill necessary for children to develop so they become independent. But autonomy needs interdependency. Though those may seem like opposite concepts, together they contribute to creating and living a healthy family life. Interdependency is one of the essential building blocks to developing autonomy because it encourages external support and a safety net; promotes healthy boundaries; and fosters self-esteem and mutual respect.

L = Quality of Family Life

Family quality of life is when each family member independently and the family as a unit has the opportunity to pursue and achieve goals individually and together.

Special Note

At the end of each chapter, I've included a section called "REAL Important Takeaways." These are the highlights of the chapter and are meant as a quick guide for you. Additionally, I have compiled all of the "REAL Important Takeaways" from each chapter into a downloadable PDF available at untamedchaosbook.com/resources so that you can have all of them in one place.

REAL Important Takeaways

Following are the five first steps in each category of REAL for you to implement in order to cultivate resilience, empowerment, autonomy, and quality of family life.

Resilience

1. Take care of yourself first. It is essential, and it is not selfish! Get plenty of sleep, practice deep breathing, nourish your body, participate in activities that you enjoy, and find ways to connect. The analogy of putting your oxygen mask on first may seem counterintuitive, especially in a crisis, but if you don't start with yourself, you risk making panicked, emotional decisions that won't serve your family system in the long run. After all, you can't pour from an empty cup.

2. Learn from your experiences and the experiences of the people around you. Take time to reflect and introspect. Think about how you handled scenarios in the past and the consequences of those choices and decisions. Did you react rather than respond? Did you act impulsively (react) out of fear, or did you stop, take a breath, consider strategies, and then answer (respond)?

3. Don't ignore your problems. Little problems just become bigger problems. Take the time to figure out what you need to do, how to do it, and then action those strategies to solve your problem (see react versus respond, above). Remember: It's okay to ask for help. In fact, it's imperative.

4. Keep the faith and remain hopeful. While you can't change what has already happened, you can change how you respond in the future. There is always another chance to try again. Everyone is perfectly imperfect.

5. Accomplish at least one thing every day. It doesn't have to be big; you just have to do something from start to finish. One way to begin your day with an accomplishment is to simply make your bed. Task one ... complete!

Empowerment

1. Be respectful and nonjudgmental. Think about how you want to be treated. You certainly don't want to be disrespected or partially/incorrectly judged.

2. Build relationships where you and your family can be vulnerable with each other and feel comfortable enough to talk openly about feelings without the fear of letting each other down.

3. Focus on your strengths and abilities as well as others' strengths and abilities. Teach yourself to recognize when you or others are struggling. Identify the signs of overwhelm. Ask for help ... offer help. Sometimes help is not through words or by proffering a solution. Sometimes it is the act of being there and letting someone know that you have their back.

4. Support and encourage everyone, especially children, in decision making. By doing this, you foster independence, improve communication, build trust, and encourage a sense of ownership and responsibility. This helps children, in particular, develop the skills and confidence needed to become responsible and capable people.

5. Respect the decisions everyone, especially children, makes about their own life. You don't have to like or even agree with the decision. When you allow children to make their

own decisions, you help them develop their decision-making muscles, build self-confidence, take ownership of their choices, and enable them to be self-reliant individuals.

Autonomy

1. Give everyone, including yourself, time, space, and grace.

2. After your children make choices and decisions, offer positive attention or support of consequences. An example of positive attention is giving *specific* praise for their behavior or for something that they have done. Rather than saying, "Good job," say, "I really appreciate that you folded the laundry today." Supporting consequences is helping your children understand the reason behind the consequence so that they can learn from it. For example, if they break the rule of no phones at the dinner table, the consequence could be taking the phone away. But rather than taking the phone away without an explanation, reiterate *why* the rule is in place. Doing this without anger is very important.

3. Allow your children to share what is on their minds without retaliation; to tell you when they are uncomfortable; and to have command over their own bodies.

4. Encourage your children to be self-motivated. One way is to set achievable goals, which allows for a sense of purpose and direction. Another way to encourage self-motivation is to model setting goals for yourself, pursuing your own interests, and having a positive attitude even during challenges (difficult, but a valuable life skill to practice for both you and them).

5. Provide your children with age-appropriate responsibilities. As they succeed, allow them more responsibility. Setting the table, feeding the dog, and putting their clean clothes away are good starting places.

Quality of Family Life

1. Respect one another.

2. Love one another unconditionally.

3. Be humble and have empathy. Say sorry when you're wrong.

4. Take responsibility for yourself and your actions.

5. Tap into spirituality. It doesn't have to be religion. It can be creative expression, meditation, practicing gratitude, or mindfulness just to name a few.

Overall, nurturing resilience, empowerment, and autonomy in children requires a combination of support, encouragement, and opportunities for growth and learning. By helping your children develop these qualities, you can help them mature into confident, capable, and successful people!

Before moving onto the next chapter, check out this chapter's corresponding activity that you can find on the resource page: untamedchaosbook.com/resources. An example of the activity and its explanation follows.

Working Journal Activity 1: From Untamed Chaos to Peace and Tranquility

To start your journey from untamed chaos to peace and tranquility, complete Activity 1 in your Working Journal with your family.

This activity allows each person, even the littles, to have a voice and to share their personal thoughts with the whole family. Try not to invalidate or get defensive as you work through this. You need about fifteen to twenty minutes; colored pencils, markers, or crayons; and colored sticky pads, like Post-its. Be as open, honest, and vulnerable as you can be.

Step 1

Take a look at the boxes, and circle three to four words that describe each one of you as individuals. Then, circle three to four words that describe your family. Little ones can play along using the feeling faces icons, which can help them express their thoughts, feelings, and emotions in an independent, self-determining way. Everybody has a voice!

THE REAL IN REAL PEACEFUL PARENTING

State of Untamed Chaos

Socially	Isolated Lonely Left Out Bullied Embarrassed Stereotyped Tantrums Helpless	Targeted Ignored Avoided Disliked Frustrated Confused Hopeless
Emotionally	Tired Depressed Angry Helpless Ashamed Embarrassed	Frustrated Tantrums Hopeless Confused Lonely
Academically	Dislikes School Embarrassed Pressured Anxious Isolated Lonely Bullied Stereotyped Tantrums Helpless	Stupid Alone Targeted Ignored Avoided Left Out Disliked Frustrated Hopeless

Feeling Faces Icons:

Joyful　　Happy　　Meh　　Sad　　Angry

Now I want you to put that paper aside. Those feelings are real! And they won't necessarily go away today or even tomorrow, but they don't have to be permanent. And they don't have to keep having a negative effect on you or your family. What you're going to do next is help change the negative soundtrack playing over and over in your head. The words you use have power, so think carefully about the vocabulary in this next part of the activity. The goal is to become aware of your thoughts so that you can change them and, in doing so, navigate your way out of the chaos.

Step 2

Now that the negative thoughts are out in the open, it's time to dream big ... really big! It's time to think about what you want your life to look like.

- How do you see yourself and your children in the future?
- Where do you want to go?
- Who do you want to share your life with?
- How do you want to feel?

Using this second list of words, circle three to four that describe the dream emotions for you and your family. Again, this should be done as a family and as individuals. For the little ones, use the feeling faces icons, pictures from magazines, and/or have them draw what they are thinking and feeling. It is very important that everyone has a voice and shares.

Creating Our Peace and Tranquility

Socially	Included Hopeful Energized Sporting Teams Community Events Invitations	Organized Strong Friends Helpful Connected
Emotionally	Excited Included Hopeful Energized Strong Focused	Supported Organized Helpful Friends Calm
Academically	Successful Hopeful Focused Organized Energized	Included Helpful Calm Supported Smart

Feeling Faces Icons:

Joyful Happy Meh Sad Angry

You're going to need those Post-it notes now. Make sure to choose colors that you like and that catch your attention. Write those dream emotions (or draw the applicable positive feeling face icon) on the Post-it notes. And put them around your home so that you can see them clearly multiple times a day! A study entitled "Paper Notebooks vs. Mobile Devices: Brain Activation Differences During Memory Retrieval" has shown that when you write something down, you are more likely to actually do it. Now is your time! Time to begin the journey of long-lasting change for yourself and your children.

Look, see, and say these positive thoughts and feelings every day multiple times a day. Believe they are possible because they are!

CHAPTER 2

The Power of Words and Positive Attention

*"Keep your face to the sunshine and
you cannot see a shadow."*
—Helen Keller

The Power of Words

Words have a powerful impact on children and their overall development. Words have the power to shape their beliefs, attitudes, and self-perception. The words you use when speaking with, about, or when correcting children can either uplift and empower them or demean and discourage them. Words of encouragement fuel confidence and problem-solving skills and foster resilience. Hurtful words (even when unintentional) damage self-esteem, inhibit growth, and create lasting emotional scars. It is important for all adults, but especially parents, to understand, recognize, and process the role words play in shaping children's lives and to use those words carefully and wisely. And when you don't (and everyone fails at this sometime) to own up to it.

The BARC System

The words you use toward and attention you give to your children often directly correlate with their behavior. Before diving deeper into your responses (your words and your attention) to their stimuli, let's discuss how to better understand their behavior.

While I was working with children who had behavior challenges in school, I was also experiencing challenging behaviors in my own home. I needed a system to easily and accurately help me keep track of multiple sets of behaviors (my own behavior in responding/reacting too). So based on a data collection tool given to me by some *really* smart people, I developed the BARC System to use in my classroom and at home. It's available to you at untamedchaosbook.com/resources.

The BARC System is an easy-to-use resource to track specific behaviors—both challenging and those you want to see again and again. BARC stands for: Before, Actual, Response/Reaction, Consequence. It works by observing what is happening *before* the actual behavior is visible, what the *actual* behavior looks like, who *responded/reacted* and how, and, finally, the *consequence* (outcome) of the situation. The BARC System allows you to keep a running record of time, date, who, what, where, and when. By tracking these, you'll likely see the makings of a pattern (especially for repeated behaviors) and, perhaps, even discern a common thread. The pattern can help you recognize and encourage desired behaviors and avoid and appropriately address challenging ones!

Positive Attention

What is positive attention? Who needs it? Why is it important?

THE POWER OF WORDS AND POSITIVE ATTENTION

Positive attention is the kind of attention that validates someone's worth, their abilities, who they are as a person, and what they are doing positively. In "parentese," the person is doing *something right*. Positive attention is typically shown through words, actions, or even gestures and communicates appreciation, admiration, and respect. The goal of positive attention is to give attention to someone for behavior you would like to see repeated and remove attention from behavior you don't want to see again. It's also the perfect opportunity to let that individual know that you are proud of the person they are and are becoming … It reminds them that you love them no matter what, and you are proud of who they are as people. (The BARC System is a good way to keep track of positive behaviors you want to see repeated as well as a good way to remind *you* to give positive attention!)

Who Needs Positive Attention?

The most common questions I get asked when I speak to parenting and teaching groups are: "Why do I have to reward or say thank you to children for doing what they are supposed to do? Do you *really* want me to congratulate children for cleaning up, for making their beds?" Yes, I do!

Take a step back, and ask yourself the following: "Do I like to be recognized for a job well done? Do I like to be validated and affirmed for my accomplishments? Do I like the feeling when someone is proud or happy about me being me?" Of course you do!

Positive attention is nice for both adults and children. Moreover, it is a simple strategy that encourages desirable behaviors while decreasing—possibly even eliminating—undesirable ones. It won't cost you a penny or demand too much of your time. And you'll rock your children's world! Best of all, you can start giving positive attention right now!

What Positive Attention Is Not

Positive attention is not simply saying "thank you" or "good job." Those phrases tell your children nothing specific about what they did to get your attention. However, when you say, "Thank you for sharing with your sister," "Great job starting that task on your own," and "I love it when you use your inside voice while I'm on the phone," you're identifying the exact reason that you are giving them positive attention. They know precisely what behavior is going to please you and cause you to pay attention to them in a very positive way. Chances are, they'll repeat that behavior again and again. In addition to verbal praise, a reward can be used to positively reinforce people of all ages. A pat on the back, a smile, a few minutes of your time … Just saying.

How to Give and Receive Positive Attention

The first step in giving positive attention is catching your children "doing good" and then offering them praise. Praise increases the positive behaviors you want them to repeat. So recognizing, through praise, exactly what behavior elicited your positive attention gives your children the first piece of the puzzle. In addition to verbal praise, giving your children hugs or high fives, listening attentively when they share their stories or concerns, and simply spending dedicated quality time together is positive attention that can be used to reinforce desired behaviors.

Positive attention also assures your children that you recognize them as people and *not* just as their behavior. When you provide positive attention, you reinforce your children's positive behaviors

THE POWER OF WORDS AND POSITIVE ATTENTION

and personality traits and, thus, encourage them to continue to develop these habits. That, in turn, contributes to the healthy development of self-concept and positive self-esteem. When your children feel loved and valued by you and believe that you are proud of the individuals they are becoming, they are more likely to see themselves in a positive way and feel confident in what they do.

When I went back to school, I remember my husband saying how proud he was that I was chasing my degree. It meant alot! Then my daughter said to me, and I quote, "I'm proud of you mom. Now maybe I can help you with your homework." I lost my mind when she said that! My heart was so full of gratitude for both of them. There are so many life lessons in that one statement. Gratitude, admiration, wisdom, kindness ... I felt all of those toward my daughter. You can live those feelings too if you just open your heart and mind to receiving positive attention.

It's time to take a step back and really look at how you give and receive attention.

Here are four things to consider when giving positive attention:

1. Be specific about what you are praising or admiring. Your children will understand exactly what they did well and can consciously and intentionally repeat it. This gives them control over their behavior. Remind them that you love them no matter what.

2. Be timely. You need to give positive attention as soon as possible after the behavior has occurred. This ensures that your children understand which behavior is being praised and makes them feel valued and appreciated. Don't forget to tell them that you are proud not only of what they have done but of who they are.

3. Be sincere and authentic. Children can tell when your praise is insincere, and this can have the opposite effect of what you intend.

4. Use a positive and enthusiastic voice to convey your admiration, your appreciation, and your joy over what your children have done (how you say something speaks volumes).

Receiving positive attention involves being open to and accepting positive feedback and recognition from others. Here are four things that will help you accept and receive positive attention.

1. Accept the compliment! When someone gives you positive attention, accept it graciously. Say "thank you," and acknowledge the person's praise for you. You are worth it!

2. Believe in yourself and in your abilities. If you have low self-esteem or you doubt your own abilities, it can be difficult to accept positive attention, but it's important to learn how to do this. Start by saying "thank you" when you get a compliment instead of brushing it off.

3. Take positive attention to heart, and internalize it. By paying attention to your own thoughts and emotions without judgment, you can replace negative thoughts and beliefs with positive thoughts and actions. This boosts your own self-confidence and motivates you. Write in a gratitude journal, practice positive self-talk, and surround yourself with positive people to internalize and accept positive attention!

4. When you receive positive attention, pay it forward. Use it as an opportunity to give positive attention to someone else. This creates a cycle of positivity and encouragement!

THE POWER OF WORDS AND POSITIVE ATTENTION

Now that you have considered these tips, write some ideas about when and with whom you'll put giving and receiving positive attention into action. More suggestions and places for you to include your written thoughts are available at untamedchaosbook.com/resources. When you write something down, you are five times more likely to follow through with it!

Why It's Important

You know that positive attention helps to build self-esteem, promotes healthy emotional development, and encourages children to repeat a particular positive behavior. In addition, positive attention strengthens the bond between family members. When parents give positive attention, they show their children that they are valued and loved for who they are rather than just for their achievements or behavior. Remember: Positive attention is not dependent only on children's behavior. You *must* recognize and provide positive attention for their personality traits, like kindness and creativity. In doing this, you will assure them that they are valued not only for their behavior but for who they are as human beings.

When you give positive attention, children reciprocate those feelings, which creates a positive cycle that strengthens family bonds.

REAL Important Takeaways

Resilience

Positive attention plays a critical role in building resilience by establishing strong relationships built on respect, which support families during the good and the challenging times.

Empowerment

By giving and receiving positive attention, you build a relationship where each member of the family feels comfortable enough to discuss their feelings and wants. They are empowered to make choices and decisions as well as understand the consequences of those decisions. By focusing on strengths and abilities rather than challenges, you maintain positivity and remain solution oriented. Of course, you shouldn't ignore challenges, but you can and will have the skills to look for a positive way to address them.

Autonomy

Positive attention builds confidence, self-esteem, and self-image. When children feel good about themselves, when they feel confident enough to say what is on their minds, when they are empowered and resilient enough to make decisions, they become independent and self-reliant … autonomous!

Quality of Family Life

Giving positive attention to your children will generally give you more positive results. When you give your attention and recognition to positive actions, your children are more likely to repeat them. Likewise, focusing only on the negative will result in more negative behavior and a more challenging family life overall. Respecting your children will empower them to feel valued and worthy. And children who feel valued and worthy respond by showing you respect. It's a cycle that will improve the quality of life within your home by fostering a supportive environment where everyone has room to grow and develop.

THE POWER OF WORDS AND POSITIVE ATTENTION

Following is an example of an activity from the Working Journal at untamedchaosbook.com/resources that will help you kick-start positive attention ideas.

Working Journal Activity 2: Positive Attention

One way to give positive attention is to "catch" your children being or doing good and praise them for it. Praise not only shows your children that you are paying attention to them but that you see and recognize the behavior that they exhibit in a good way.

Remember: When you praise your children, you need to tell them exactly what they have done well. You want them to repeat the behavior, so it is important that they understand how to do so. Praise such as, "Thank you for putting your laundry in the hamper," "You did a great job raking the leaves," or "Thank you for taking the dog for a walk around the block" is specific and easy to understand. A little bit of recognition, appreciation, and thanks can go a long way!

Now jot down some key phrases that you can use to give your children positive attention. Need inspiration? Consider what you would want to hear about you. Ask your children what they'd like to hear! What do they want you to see? More importantly, what do they want you to say? You may even want to stick this list on the refrigerator where everyone can see it so that every family member can start this practice.

_____

_____

_____

CHAPTER 3

With Big Choices and Decisions Come BIG Emotions

"One day your child will make a mistake or a bad choice and run to you instead of away from you and in that moment you will know the immense value of peaceful, positive, respectful parenting."
—L.R.Knost

But mom ... I want cake for breakfast!

Control—such a strong and oftentimes intimidating word. Being in control means having authority or power over someone or something. It means making decisions and taking actions that influence the outcome of a situation. Most often you, as a parent, are the "authority" in your family and have the control to make decisions that affect the entire family. The bigger the decision, the bigger the emotional stake.

This is especially true for parents when you have to make the big decision to give your children control over some decision making. I'm not suggesting that you give up total control (your own big emotions might be rising right now at the thought of this). But I want you to imagine giving your children control of ...

something. Still struggling with the idea? Take a deep breath … Let it out slowly. Here's a few more questions to consider.

- Do you like to be in control?
- Make your own choices?
- Make your own decisions?

According to a 2007 study entitled "The 200 Daily Food Decisions We Overlook," by researchers Brian Wansink and Jeffery Sobal at Cornell University, adults make an average of 35,000 decisions every single day. Roughly 220 of those decisions are about food!

How did you learn to make those 35,000 daily decisions? Through a lifetime of practice! As an adult, you have control over your home, choices you make at work, and choices you make in your personal life. You've made millions of choices and decisions, both easy and difficult. Right? Think about that.

Even as a child, you made some choices and decisions on your own, like which book to take out of the library or which page to color in the coloring book … or to color on the living room wall. That was the beginning of your decision-making muscle building! As you got older, your choices and decisions became complicated, more impactful. Even life-changing. You decided to study or not study for a test. You chose to smoke or to not smoke. You chose to drink that beer or to not drink that beer. Ultimately, you made bigger and more difficult (and, hopefully, good, solid, and safe) decisions as you matured. If you made a "bad" choice or decision, ideally, you learned from it and didn't do it again. In all, you've made millions of small decisions throughout your life. You had control over what you did or ate or wore and got better and better at making decisions. You built your decision-making muscles and didn't even know you were doing it.

WITH BIG CHOICES AND DECISIONS COME BIG EMOTIONS

Now you need to help your children build their decision-making muscles too.

Still a bit uncomfortable with the idea of giving control to your children? I was. The question is: *Why* are you uncomfortable giving your children control?

An article from the Child Mind Institute, "Helping Kids Make Decisions" (childmind.org/article/helping-kids-make-decisions/), presents several reasons why parents won't give control to their children that are consistent with my own experiences from speaking with families and even within my own family.

First, many parents retain all decision-making control because they are afraid that their children will make the wrong decision and fail at something. They want to protect their children from the disappointment of negative consequences.

Second are cultural or generational differences when it comes to decision making. In some cultures and generations, children are not encouraged to make decisions or to have control over anything in their lives.

Third, parents have a total lack of trust in their children's judgment and decision-making skills and feel more comfortable making decisions for them.

Fourth, parents are too busy or stressed to take the time or don't have the energy to involve the children in the decision-making process. They take the easy way out and make the decisions for their children (this one hits *very* close to home for my family).

And fifth ... drum roll please ... I believe, based on my own experiences, that the biggest reason parents feel uncomfortable giving their children control is because they feel they are losing control. Whoa! But they aren't actually losing control by giving their children control. They are keeping it. The children just don't realize it! Let me explain.

While it's difficult to let go of control, giving your children the opportunity to make choices and decisions helps them develop important life skills, such as time management, self-esteem, negotiation skills, and problem-solving. Most importantly, allowing decisions and giving control helps them build their independence. You're going to gradually increase your children's control and decision making over time. By doing this, you build trust and confidence in their ability to make good choices. In essence, you're retaining control over the process of them learning and growing into their independence.

Making choices and decisions has a learning curve. The more choices or decisions you (and your children) make, the better you and they will become at making choices and decisions. Think about that for a moment. If you never let your children decide what to wear, or choose what to eat, or decide what to do first, how are they going to make good choices later in life? They won't know how to!

My husband and I learned this the hard way. Because we did not allow our son to make some basic decisions on his own (we didn't trust him to make good choices), when it came time to choose between doing something right or wrong, for example, smoking on the school bus, he consistently made poor decisions.

On the other hand, we learned from that and allowed our daughter to make more decisions independently. By the time she was in high school, she was making more good, solid decisions than poor decisions. For example, she was invited to a party. There was drinking. She called and asked me to pick her up.

WITH BIG CHOICES AND DECISIONS COME BIG EMOTIONS

Reality check: You are not giving them control over the car or your bank account. You are giving them enough control over a *personal* decision that they can build their decision-making muscles.

Remember: By allowing children to make choices and decisions and giving them age-appropriate control over their own person, you are helping them to:

1. Build confidence and self-esteem. Having control shows them that their opinion and their preferences matter and that they are capable of making good choices.

2. Develop problem-solving skills. By practicing and building their decision-making muscles, children learn how to look at all their options and make an informed decision.

3. Foster independence. Decision making teaches them how to take responsibility for their actions, face consequences, and navigate the world around them.

4. Cultivate self-motivation. Having control increases their motivation because they are more invested in the outcome.

Here's the rub: Giving control can set off big emotions not only for you as a parent, but for your children as well. It's important to help them understand and harness those big emotions. First, validate your children's feelings, and let them know that their feelings are okay and healthy. Saying things like, "I know you are disappointed that you can't spend time with your friends," lets them know that you hear and understand their sadness and frustration. It also helps them label their big emotions, which allows them to develop their emotional intelligence.

Why Are Big Emotions BIG?

Sometimes, when children get the control and power to make their own choices, they make poor ones. Why? Because emotions get the better of them. In his book *Emotional Intelligence*, Daniel Goleman introduces the term "amygdala hijack," which means having a fight-or-flight response that is out of proportion to a common stimulus, like making a decision. Fight-or-flight pushes the body to an immediate action and activates big emotions. When this happens, those big emotions, such as stress, anger, and fear, come to the fore and override reasoning and logical thinking as well as problem-solving skills. As a result, without thinking about or considering the potential consequences, your children act impulsively.

Things might get thrown, you might get yelled at, doors might slam. But all is not lost! When this happens, validate their big emotions and feelings (and yours!), and let them know that you are there to help them get through it. The immediate goal is to establish calm. This is the time to give them a choice like "I'm here, and you may sit down and talk to me about this, or you may sit someplace quietly until you feel calmer."

The most important step in this emotional processing practice is to have a space for them to calm down. Once your children have experienced the big emotion, give them their choice, and provide a safe space. Consider sitting them on the couch or perhaps even just on a step. For older children, consider allowing them to go to their room.

One of my favorite calming spaces was a special chair that I called the "Be Nice Chair." I used this chair in my classrooms, with private clients, and at home. When the children were having big emotions, they went and sat in that chair until they calmed down and were able to join in again. Eventually, the children would ask to go to the chair and sit ... before the behavior got out of control! I share this strategy with teachers and parents whenever I have the chance because it is simple and easy to implement and ... *it works*!

Some big emotions may be too much even for a calming space. Big emotions may come out as tantrums or meltdowns. And they don't just happen with children. You've seen them ... in the grocery store, on the playground, on the Little League field. And boy do those adults look ... Well, you know how they look!

Tantrums and Meltdowns

When children are disappointed by a choice or decision they have made, and the outcome is not what they expected, they may toss a tantrum or have a meltdown. This is a natural response to feeling overwhelmed by challenging emotions. It's their way of saying to you, "I don't understand this, help me understand." Tantrums and meltdowns are very often a way for children to try to communicate their feelings and what they want when they can't find the words. By listening to them and acknowledging their emotions, you help them feel heard, validated, and valued.

Tantrums and meltdowns are a chance for everyone, but particularly your children, to learn how to manage those big emotions. Moreover, when you model calm and respect, you teach your children how to cope with those big emotions in a healthy way. This is where emotional intelligence for all family members comes into play.

Emotional intelligence, by its simplest definition, is understanding and using emotions effectively. With emotional intelligence, children and adults are able to build relationships and make better decisions as well as navigate social situations. Emotional intelligence does not develop overnight. It is a lifelong process for everyone.

A Starting Strategy to Build Decision-Making Muscles

Here is one very easy strategy to implement decision-making opportunities for your children.

Give them a choice of two or three options—"Which of these do you want/this or that?" Why? Because you'll still have control over their choices while giving them the opportunity to feel like they are in control of themselves. Too many choices leads to more confusion.

For example: Do you want the orange popsicle, the red popsicle, or a snowcone? Do you want to read, draw, or play a board game? Do you want carrots, brussels sprouts, or green beans for dinner?

As your children get older, allow them to make more meaningful decisions, but try to always offer options. For example: Do you want to spend your allowance on candy and magazines, a new pair of sneakers, or do you just want to keep saving it?

REAL Important Takeaways

Resilience

By allowing children to make decisions and choices, you help them develop the problem-solving skills that are important for resilience. When children are given the opportunity to make decisions, they learn how to thoughtfully look at all their options, weigh the pros and cons, and make informed choices. Thus, they can better navigate the challenges and setbacks that will occur in life.

Empowerment

When children can make decisions and choices and have control over their person, they feel more empowered. They know that their opinions, ideas, and preferences matter and that they have a say in their own lives as well as the life of the family. It increases their self-esteem and confidence and helps them to develop a sense of self-control.

Autonomy

Allowing children control to make decisions helps them to become autonomous. When children have control over part of their lives, they practice their decision-making and problem-solving skills. They become capable of making informed decisions and navigating mistakes. And as they approach their teens and young adult years, they are prepared to make bigger and better decisions.

Quality of Family Life

Allowing children to make decisions and choices creates a sense of cooperation and collaboration within the family, which builds trust and opens up communication between you and your children. This fosters a supportive family environment.

Making decisions and choices inevitably leads to consequences. The next chapter discusses consequences and why it is important that your children—and you—understand them. If you haven't yet downloaded the Working Journal, please do that now at untamedchaosbook.com/resources.

Working Journal Activity 3: With Big Choices and Decisions Come BIG Emotions

Do you like to be in control? To be free to make your own choices? Make your own decisions? So do your children! So help them build their decision-making muscles. The more choices and decisions they make, the better they will become at making them. They will also get practice handling the emotions that come with the consequences of their own decisions.

Relinquishing decision-making control is really hard for adults in many cases. But if you don't allow your children to make their own decisions and choices in some areas in their lives (areas that don't affect their safety, for example), they will never grow those decision-making muscles.

Hint: Early on, give them limited choices—a "which one of these" option, like "Which veggie do you want for dinner: corn, green beans, or carrots?" Why? Because your children will feel some control while you ultimately maintain control. In this example, you are saying they need to have a veggie (yeah for you!) while simultaneously giving them the power to make a choice.

But beware of giving them a "yes" or "no" choice if "no" is not really an option. Please be thoughtful as you give your children the opportunity to make choices and decisions.

Following, start a list of decisions and choices that you feel safe allowing your children to make right now. Use your Working Journal for more space.

UNTAMED CHAOS

CHAPTER 4

The Good, the Bad, the Reality: Understanding and Accepting Consequences

"To succeed, you need to find something to hold on to, something to motivate you, something to inspire you."
—Tony Dorsett

Consequences are important because they influence the choices you make and shape your behaviors. They contribute to teaching life skills, like responsibility, accountability, and understanding cause and effect so that you can make more intentional decisions. The more decisions you make and the more consequences you experience, the better you become at making decisions and understanding and accepting their consequences.

Helping children understand and accept consequences can be one of the most challenging steps for you as a parent (and for your children too). But the *consequences* of moving forward on this path from untamed chaos to peace and tranquility are astonishing. Keep going! Yes, I said the consequences are astonishing! You're in disbelief: "How can consequences be astonishing?" Ahhhh, Grasshopper … let me show you.

What Are Consequences?

Often consequences are seen as a way of shaping a child's behavior by providing incentives for positive behavior and discouraging negative behavior through punishment.

Through this lens, consequences sound pretty bad.

Fortunately, that is not true. A consequence, simply put, is the result or outcome that follows a particular activity, action, or behavior. It can be positive, negative, or neutral. If it's pouring rain and you go outside with your umbrella, you stay dry (as long as you put it up!). That's a positive consequence! You sow a seed, a plant grows. You clean the house, you feel good, and the house looks amazing! Those are all consequences and good ones at that!

But you won't always like the results of a decision you make. You dye your hair purple … and it looks hideous (at least on my head it does!). You eat a gallon of ice cream, you get a belly ache (not that I know from personal experience or anything). You see what I'm getting at, right? As an adult, in general, you understand what the consequence of a decision is going to be. You know this because you've had a lifetime of making choices, and you have survived their consequences even when you didn't like the outcome!

Learning About Consequences

Understanding consequences is vital for your children because it helps them develop a connection between their actions and behaviors and the results of those actions and behaviors. When they recognize that their actions have consequences, your children are better able to understand the impact of those actions and behaviors on themselves and others around them.

Understanding consequences helps your children develop empathy and respect for others, which are essential social skills that will impact the relationships they develop over their lifetime. When they recognize that their actions have positive or negative impacts on other people, they're more likely to take the feelings and needs of others into consideration when they make their choices and decisions. This cultivates their self-awareness and their awareness of others.

By learning about and understanding consequences, children make better decisions about what they do and how they act. They can see various possible outcomes, which helps them develop a sense of responsibility and accountability.

But in order for them to actually experience the consequences of their choices, you must allow natural consequences to unfold and not protect your children from them. You have to let them choose, decide, succeed, and fail at what they do. Intervening in the natural consequences will hinder their growth. They must fall down and figure out how to get back up again!

The Good, the Bad, the Reality

Modeling is a crucial way to demonstrate appropriate behavior when responding to a consequence that you're unhappy with. Remember, your children see and hear everything you do, so if you experience a consequence with anger or aggression, they're going to imitate that behavior. They're going to assume that anger or aggression is the correct way to deal with negative consequences. However, if you respond calmly and respectfully, if you give consideration to your response rather than reacting, they are more likely to imitate that positive behavior.

The greatest advantage of modeling appropriate response behaviors is that it builds trust with your children. They see that you are human, that you make mistakes, that you also have big emotions, *and* that you can manage them and survive whatever you're feeling. Your children are much more likely to talk to you and maybe even ask for help and guidance when they feel stuck if you model how to accept and understand consequences.

Here's some food for thought about consequences.

- What is the consequence of my choice/decision?
- Who is this going to affect?
- When will this happen?
- Can I accept and live with that outcome?

Let's look at examples of choices, decisions, and their consequences. I think some of these are funny—certainly the story about Grandpa and his fancy pants is … But I'll let you decide!

Scrambled Versus Over Easy

I remember a time when I was a child, and my mom asked me if I wanted my eggs scrambled or over easy. To this day, I love my eggs over easy. But for some unknown reason on that day, I responded that I wanted them scrambled. I remember the look of surprise on my mother's face, and she asked me if I was sure. I gave her the affirmative head nod. I think I looked at her like she was nuts. But she cooked my eggs exactly how I asked for them and gave them to me scrambled. My response was … wait for it … "But I wanted them over easy. I don't like scrambled eggs."

My mom calmly (because she is calm about almost everything) reminded me that I said I wanted scrambled eggs. I started to argue with her, but she simply responded with, "It's scrambled eggs or nothing." After some tears, whining, and pouting, I ate my eggs scrambled. All these years later, I can still recall the "incident." From that point on, I was more careful when answering my mom when she gave me a choice.

My mom knew that it was important that I stick to my choice. She knew that I would learn a lesson from having to face and accept the consequence of making a poor choice. In this case, she knew I wasn't going to starve. You need to act likewise. Give your children a choice, and then follow through with it. They may be hungry for a while or have to eat scrambled eggs, but they will manage and learn an important lesson about the cause and effect of consequences along the way.

To Pack Lunch or to Buy Lunch … That Is the Question

I used to give my daughter the option to buy lunch at school two times a week. On the other three days, she had to have a packed lunch. One terrible Monday morning, she left her lunch on the counter, so she had to buy lunch at school that day, and they were not serving something that she liked. Having to buy lunch that day meant that she only had one more lunch that she could buy during that week. So she had to choose between her two favorite school lunches on Wednesday and Friday. Needless to say, she was not happy about having to pack her lunch on pizza day!

But, ultimately, we had a winner-winner chicken dinner moment! Having learned from her consequence of missing pizza day, Kristen made the very grown-up decision to start packing her lunch the night before and putting a note on the front door to remind her to get her lunch before she left for the bus!

Fancy + Fancy = Eyesore: A Quick Story

My grandpa was a house painter, so he typically wore coveralls. But when he came home, he would change into a shirt and a pair of slacks. The problem? He always wore a striped shirt with plaid pants. Oh my goodness! It was a lot on the eyes! We created a simple rule for Grandpa to follow when picking out his clothes. He was allowed to wear a fancy shirt with plain pants, a plain shirt with fancy pants, or a plain shirt and plain pants. But *never* a fancy shirt and fancy pants! He still struggled to match the colors, but the rule worked out pretty well. At least the shirts and pants were easier on the eyes. You too can give such choices limited in scope to your children!

REAL Important Takeaways

Resilience

When your children understand and accept the consequences of their actions, they are more likely to take responsibility for their mistakes and learn from them. This, in turn, fosters resilience and enables them to practice recovering from the consequences of poor decisions (i.e., let them fall down and figure out how to get back up).

Empowerment

When children understand and accept consequences, they feel empowered as individuals because they are more in control of their own choices. They can take responsibility for their actions and behaviors instead of blaming others. The best part is they are learning from their mistakes. This is true for you too. Let me say it once more: Fall down, get back up, try again.

Autonomy

By allowing your children to make choices and decisions, you are giving them the opportunity to experience the consequences of those decisions in a safe space (because you will always do your best to support them). They have the safety and the space to experiment, explore, and make sense of their choices and the consequences.

Quality of Family Life

Giving your children positive attention and the freedom to make choices and then helping them to understand the consequences of those choices demonstrates respect and trust in your children. You are also giving them the opportunity to trust you. They can trust that, no matter what, you will have their back. You can't simply rescue them from their predicaments, but you'll be there to support them where you can.

Following, you will find an example of the next activity in your Working Journal (that hopefully you have downloaded from untamedchaosbook.com/resources).

Working Journal Activity 4: Consequences

Consequences are everywhere. They are positive, negative, and neutral. Understanding what consequences might look like for the choices each family member makes will be important in order for you to support each other.

Refer back to the choices and decisions options from the previous chapter's activity. Now make a list of consequences, both positive and not so positive, of those options.

Why are you doing this? Simply so that everyone is on the same page. Everyone is aware of and understands the consequences of certain choices.

_____

_____

_____

_____

_____

_____

_____

CHAPTER 5

Strike a Pose: React or Respond

"It is easier to build strong children than to repair broken men."
—Frederick Douglass

I'm sure you've seen, maybe you've even been, "that" parent on the ballfield. You know the one I'm talking about. The one who doesn't like the call the umpire made, the one who loses their mind, the one who yells and screams, the one who makes a scene, and the one who, ultimately, gets ejected from the game.

This chapter is about you—it's a reality check on your emotional control. You've had big emotions at some point and perhaps even behaved badly. But it's time that you become aware and intentional in your actions toward your children's behavior. When their behavior elicits big emotions, you have two choices: You can react or you can respond.

You're giving your children control over choices and helping them build their decision-making muscles. You're teaching them about cause and effect and how each of their decisions has a consequence—positive, negative, or neutral. Now it's time to model how to work through the emotions that come along with negative consequences.

Reacting and Responding

Okay, so what are reacting and responding?

Reacting is immediate and instinctual feedback to an external situation (notice I didn't say response). It happens without thought and can be driven by emotions such as fear, anger, or frustration. When you react, crazy fast messages are sent to the part of the brain called the amygdala (think of the amygdala hijack from Chapter 3). The amygdala then unleashes the stress response in your body, which makes you act impulsively, without thinking. When you react, you don't weigh the possible consequences of your actions.

Responding, on the other hand, is a mindful way of handling a situation. The prefrontal cortex (the most evolved part of the human brain), which is the decision-making headquarters, takes over. The brain takes the time between the trigger and the response to logically consider the situation, assess emotions, and choose an appropriate course of action. Responding is a deliberate approach to problem-solving and often leads to more positive outcomes.

Again, reacting is more immediate and emotionally driven while responding is more mindful and deliberate.

Keep in mind that both reacting and responding can be appropriate depending on the situation. Take a look.

STRIKE A POSE: REACT OR RESPOND

To Respond or React, That Is the Question

You are in the grocery store. Your children want the biggest, the crunchiest, the most sugar-filled cereal on the planet, and you say, "ummm … No." They toss a tantrum like you are refusing to feed them. What do you do? Do you react or do you respond?

In this situation, I would *respond*. If you react impulsively, you will probably make the situation worse. You'd likely be reacting from shame—shame that everyone in the store thinks you're a mean parent, shame that you can't control your children, shame that you aren't good enough—rather than responding from self-control.

I've lived this very situation with my daughter. She wanted something from the store, I can't even remember what, but when my answer was "No," she boo-hooed like a pro. Tears, screeching, snot … everywhere. I tried to reason with her for about two seconds and realized that was not going to work. So I pulled up my bootstraps (and tucked my shame away), and I took the shopping cart with the screaming child to the customer service desk. I picked up my daughter, told the clerk behind the desk that I was leaving the cart there, and asked them to please put the food back on the shelves. The clerk looked slightly confused, but as I carried said screaming child out the door, several other parents looked at me and clapped. In fact, one older shopper said, "Way to go, mom!"

I continued to walk calmly out to the car, and by the time my daughter was buckled into her carseat, she was begging to go back into the store, promising that she would stop crying. We did not go back into the store. We went home without any groceries. She felt the consequences of her actions, and I felt the power of maintaining self-control. Needless to say, she never threw a tantrum in the grocery store again.

Here is another example. You're in the front yard, and your child chases a ball into the street. Do you respond or do you react?

In this scenario, you react! Without even blinking or thinking, you grab your child by the shoulders and pull them back to safety as the bus speeds past. That's not a bad thing! Not at all! You did it without thinking, which is the evolutionary purpose of reacting.

Human beings need to be able to react to threats without conscious thought because taking the time to respond can end in tragedy in urgent situations. There is a time and a place for both reacting and responding, and once you are able to work on your awareness of them, you will have more control over your life.

What You Say

I am a Disney freak, so I like to use examples from the movies. Thumper, the bunny in *Bambi*, says it best: "If you can't say something nice, don't say nothing at all." Well, who hasn't broken that rule?! When you experience big emotions, it's hard to stop and breathe and *think* before saying anything.

But when reacting or responding, the words you choose can have a significant impact on the outcome. And it isn't always the actual words you use but *how* you use those words that matters most. Here are some words and phrases that can be used when both reacting and responding that are not hurtful.

Reacting

- Stop!
- No!
- Don't do that!

STRIKE A POSE: REACT OR RESPOND

- That's not okay!
- That's not safe!

Responding

- I understand how you feel.
- Let's work together to find a solution.
- Can you tell me more about what is going on?
- I hear what you're saying.
- I'm sorry you feel that way.
- Let's take a deep breath, and think this through.

Do you see how these reacting and responding words can keep your children safe and help them through uncomfortable situations, respectively, without being hurtful?

What You Do

Very often, anger and fear surface when you perceive something as dangerous or threatening. This initial reaction puts you into fight-or-flight mode—either defensive or like deer in the headlights. The amygdala sends messages throughout the body to get ready to fight, to freeze, or to flee. You get tense, and your heart rate might go up.

How many times have you been so angry that you weren't sure what you were going to do? You are not alone. This is when you practice taking a pause to transition from reacting to *responding* (unless you or the child is in imminent danger). Remember the thinking part of the brain, the prefrontal cortex, the part of the brain that helps you plan, make decisions, and regulate emotions? Use it. Stop, take a breath, and think before you say or do something that you can't take back. Harming children or even another adult is not appropriate. You can say something to calm yourself down like, "I need a minute before we continue this conversation." Walking away is another appropriate response, as is counting to ten, or taking ten deep breaths—whatever you need to do to give yourself enough time for your thinking brain to kick in.

There are special little neurons in your brain called mirror neurons. And they are just that, a mirror. They respond, or fire off, when you act or behave in a specific way and when you see someone else acting or behaving in a similar manner. Why are these little critters important? Well, they enable you to learn through observation to imitate and copy someone else's actions and behaviors. Thus, they play a vital role in learning socially appropriate behaviors as well as inappropriate behaviors! Your children's mirror neurons mirror *your* behavior. Keeping this in mind can help you model being a superhero or a supervillain. Which do you want to model for your children?

Do you do any of the following when you react or respond?

Reacting

- Physically move away from a dangerous situation.
- Yell or raise your voice to express anger, fear, or frustration.
- Criticize or blame.
- Jump to conclusions and make assumptions.
- Use physical force to stop a behavior.

Responding

- Offer support, empathy, and validation.
- Work with others to find a solution that benefits everyone.
- Identify and express emotions in a calm and respectful way.

- Listen and understand another person's perspective.
- Make sure that boundaries are clear, and express your needs respectfully.

I don't know about you, but I can actually *feel* the difference between these two forms of feedback. Like I said, in some situations, reacting is the best choice, and, sometimes, raising your voice or grabbing your children is necessary to keep them safe. But when that is not the situation, you can see how reacting rather than responding could be dangerous, right?

I will say this again … and again … and probably again. Your children see and hear everything you say and do, and they mimic everything that you say and do. It's important to remember that both reacting and responding can be correct in different situations. The key is to choose actions and words that are respectful, constructive, and appropriate to the situation. You, as the parent, know which situation calls for which feedback. Don't expect your children to understand that if you haven't taught it to them. To build stronger and more positive relationships, it's imperative to think about how you can be a positive role model for your children by responding and reacting at the appropriate times.

REAL Important Takeaways

Resilience

Responding effectively to challenges models the problem-solving and coping skills that build resilience. Being calm and thoughtful encourages children to develop that skill themselves. By modeling socially appropriate actions and behaviors and being a good example, you positively influence your children's behavior.

Empowerment

Allowing your children to make choices and have some control over what is going on around them can help them feel empowered. Responding to your children in a way that validates their input, ideas, and perspectives encourages empowerment.

Autonomy

Knowing how and when to react versus respond empowers your children to make choices and decisions for themselves. When your children have the space and opportunity to make their own decisions, they cultivate their feelings of independence and build their decision-making muscles and problem-solving skills.

Quality of Family Life

By understanding the importance of consequences and modeling the appropriate reactions and responses, families build trust and mutual respect. When everyone responds from a place of control, there is less fighting and more intention.

The next chapter covers routines, flexible scheduling, and teachable moments. No, you're not going to jampack the schedule so tight that there's no wiggle room for fun or serendipity. No, you're not going to allow the children to create the daily schedule so that it's like having a slumber party all day long. And, yes, I'll cover those moments that pop up when you can teach something unexpected. Those moments are some of the greatest teaching opportunities that you, as a parent, can experience!

STRIKE A POSE: REACT OR RESPOND

But first, try out the next activity that can be found in the Working Journal at untamedchaosbook.com/resources. It's an opportunity to consider appropriate situations for reacting and responding.

Working Journal Activity 5: React Versus Respond

Following are two columns of words and a chart. One column on the chart is "React," and the other is "Respond." Your assignment, if you choose to accept it, is to match each word with the action of reacting or responding. Quick review: When you react, you typically do it without thinking. When you respond, you typically take the time to think about what you are going to do and why. Keep in mind that reacting and responding can both be positive depending on the situation.

Immediate danger	Time sensitive
Violate your boundaries	Safety
Emotional triggers	Non-emergency
Multiple options	Need for diplomacy
High emotions	Physical harm
Defending yourself	Defending someone else

React	Respond

CHAPTER 6

Routine Versus Flexible Schedule

"You may never know what results come of your actions, but if you do nothing, there will be no results."
—Mahatma Gandhi

Okay, you've given your children control over a personal matter, you've given them positive attention, you've supported them through consequences, and you are modeling reactions versus responses. And now ... Now you're going to let your children make the daily schedule?! "Okay, sure. Dr. Teri, this is what our day would look like: Sleep until noon or eyes pop open just as the sun is peeking over the horizon; Captain Crunch for breakfast followed by a serving of ice cream with chocolate syrup; then twelve hours of video games, Disney channel, and screen time. Dinner? Let's have ... cake and maybe more ice cream ... more video games ... dancing to loud music. And now it's late, we are exhausted, and the children decide it is time to go to bed, only to schedule this all again for tomorrow!"

No, this is not what I am suggesting. That sounds like a slumber party, and, well, life is not a slumber party!

First let's talk about routine and flexible scheduling. On paper, routine and flexible scheduling appear to be totally opposite.

Routine involves planning specific times for certain activities on a regular basis. It provides structure and predictability, which is beneficial for most people. Having a routine can help establish a set of healthy habits that contribute to your overall well-being.

Flexible scheduling, on the other hand, is a more fluid approach to planning. There is much less emphasis on specific time and more focus on flexibility and adaptability. There tends to be more freedom, which allows for more autonomy and for life to happen on its own terms without the stress of trying to stick to a rigid routine when it's not possible. Some people find that flexible scheduling helps to reduce stress, increase creativity, and allow more opportunities to explore new things.

Both routine and flexible scheduling have their benefits and drawbacks depending on the needs of you and your family. I personally benefit from a combination of both approaches. In fact, a combination also worked well in our home and in the classrooms where I taught.

Creating a Flexible Schedule/Routine

Creating a flexible schedule that simultaneously includes routine is kind of a balancing act. Predictability and structure are beneficial not only to your children but to you too, especially when you are trying to keep big emotions in check. Here's the thing: Having a bit of flexibility in that schedule is vitally important because life happens, things come up, and if you are too rigid with the schedule, those big emotions will come out, and you'll make poor choices. So having certain routines with flexibility built in is the best of both approaches.

ROUTINE VERSUS FLEXIBLE SCHEDULE

Even when you have a fixed schedule or routine, something at sometime is going to change, and you will need to deal with it. That might be a real challenge for you, so while you might not like it, it's a good idea to learn how to handle those "unexpected" events. Besides, sometimes those unexpected moments turn into excellent learning opportunities!

No Surprises! And Yet ...

It's important that the family expectations (more about expectations in an upcoming chapter) include some kind of routine, which builds consistency and helps to create calm, predictability, and a sense of control.

Consistency is essential for all children, especially those with challenging behaviors. Children typically thrive on predictability, yet a rigid or inflexible routine can be a source of unnecessary stress. Let me give you an example. In one class I taught, I was instructed to put a daily schedule on the chalkboard. (Yes, a chalkboard! I taught when dinosaurs still roamed the Earth.) I would list all of the activities and the *times* for each one to the minute. Our schedule looked something like this: morning meeting at 9:00–9:15, math at 9:15–10:00, bathroom break at 10:00–10:05, reading at 10:05–11:45. You get the idea. Here was the problem: If we were working on math and we ran over time, the children would lose their minds! They panicked because of not finishing on time and then starting something else late (because it was beyond their understanding). I remember one student crying because we were still working on math, but it was time for reading, and we were going to be late. It got to the point where I simply wrote the tasks on the chalkboard but not the times. As we moved from one task to another, we would erase it from the board. It was easier to tell them that we would work until we were finished or, better yet, at a good spot to stop.

This was much more effective. The children didn't feel pressured to complete a task in a given time, which allowed each one to work at their own pace and not be expected to perform according to a generalized standard. I was also able to adapt to the teachable moments. I could stop, respond, adapt, teach, and then bring them back to the task at hand.

These kinds of moments reveal themselves throughout the day, and I encourage you to recognize the shift in the routine. Understand that your children may exhibit some strong feelings, and you will need to recognize and adapt. Being flexible allows you to address issues as they arise and not put them off or avoid them. Modeling flexibility teaches children to be flexible. Some children are more flexible than others (just like adults!), but when children feel safe and secure—secure with the change and safe to feel whatever they are going to feel—they learn they can roll with the punches so to speak. The more experiences children have with a flexible schedule, the less stress and/or anxiety they will feel, and they will learn to be more in control of their emotions and behaviors.

Here are suggestions for incorporating routine with flexible scheduling:

1. Identify priorities; these are what must be completed. They are key activities that are important to the individual and the family, like school and sport commitments, meal times, exercise, and work. Plan a routine around these priorities, but allow for flexibility and adjustments as things come up.

2. Build in a buffer. Allow for extra time between activities so that when something unexpected happens or delays occur, you'll have a buffer so activities don't crash together. This reduces stress and allows for more flexibility in your schedule.

ROUTINE VERSUS FLEXIBLE SCHEDULE

3. Create a visual schedule. Include both the routine activities and the flexible spots. Be sure to include the *must-dos* and the *want-to-dos* too.

4. Include your children in the planning and decision-making process. This is an opportunity for them to share their interests and their preferences.

5. Incorporate teachable moments. Turn an unexpected event or a disruption into a teachable moment. Use everyday experiences and challenges as an opportunity to learn and grow. When unexpected events arise, talk to your children about what's happened and their feelings around the unexpected change, and work through the change together.

Ah, the teachable moment. You know they're going to pop up, and you're never quite ready for them, but that's okay. Everyone can benefit from a teachable moment. Even you! So what is a teachable moment?

A teachable moment is an event, experience, or question that appears and presents an opportunity to teach something that was not necessarily planned or expected. They happen often when your children ask you a question or something happens in your schedule that you didn't expect. One of the many cool things about a teachable moment is that they give you the perfect opportunity to model decision making, accepting consequences, reacting versus responding, and flexibility!

The ability to go with the flow and adapt to changes physically, emotionally, and behaviorally is a lifelong skill that continues to evolve throughout adulthood. You may have heard this referred to as one of the "soft skills," non-technical skills that encompass emotional intelligence, social understanding, and communication that enable people to basically get along. Teachable moments can be the most natural way to encourage and support soft skills. They can open the door for conversation or even spontaneous activity.

I remember right after I started teaching (back in the Dark Ages … when we wrote on rocks), there was an event that happened in the news, and my students came to school very upset. There was a bombing on foreign soil that impacted our military. Many of the children in my class came from military families and were watching important adults in their life go overseas. Many were frightened that even I (an important adult) would have to go too. One student after another came into the classroom frightened, asking questions about what had happened. Rather than spending the morning teaching reading, rather than worrying about the multiplication tables that I was planning to teach, I spent the morning answering all their questions and discussing what had happened. I helped them process their feelings around the event and feel validated. I allowed the schedule to be flexible that day. Lunchtime came and went. My students came back to the classroom, sat down, and were ready to read and even do some multiplication tables. I consider that day to have been a perfect teachable moment.

Imagine you plan to picnic with your children at lunchtime, but it starts raining. The children are disappointed, and there are some big emotions coming out. You can use this as a moment to say something like, "We can't sit outside and have a picnic, but let's spread a blanket out in the family room and have our picnic there! We can look out the windows and watch the rain while we have our lunch." It's not the same thing as having a picnic in the yard or at the park, but it's definitely more fun sitting on a blanket having lunch than sitting at the boring old kitchen table!

Speaking of the kitchen table, let's talk about homework.

ROUTINE VERSUS FLEXIBLE SCHEDULE

Homework, the Bane of a Parent's Existence

One of the hottest topics that comes up during my private small group coaching sessions is homework. Let me start by saying that I feel your pain, your frustration, and your desire to throw in the towel. Your children come home with that "Everyday Math" or a task to read a text and then analyze what they've read. "This little piggy went to market, this little piggy stayed home, this little piggy had roast beef, this little piggy had none, this little piggy went wee wee wee all the way home." Why did the piggy stay home? Why did only one piggy have roast beef? Did the cow jump over the moon before or after the piggy ran home? You know the feeling! If your children take five hours to do homework, it is too long! Do they really have to do *that* much homework?

This is a good time to take a deep dive, and, for goodness sake, talk to their teacher. *Yes*! Talk to the teacher first. Do not go to the administration before speaking with your most informed and direct source of up-to-date information about your children. If you don't get any satisfaction, put your request in writing to the teacher and perhaps copy the counselor or even the principal (create a paper trail). But don't jump to the top of the chain until you have attempted to speak with the teacher directly.

Before going any further, I would like to provide some guidance from two groups of experts. The National Education Association (NEA) and the National Parent Teacher Association (NPTA) *both* support the ten-minute homework rule: Children should have no more than ten minutes of homework each day based on their current grade. This is not written in stone, but it is a guideline set by two groups of experts who (I firmly believe) know, understand, and have your children's best interest at heart.

1st	10 minutes	7th	70 minutes
2nd	20 minutes	8th	80 minutes
3rd	30 minutes	9th	90 minutes
4th	40 minutes	10th	100 minutes
5th	50 minutes	11th	110 minutes
6th	60 minutes	12th	120 minutes

These are simply guidelines, and the amount of homework for each grade in every district in every state can be different. In many cases, the homework policy can be found on your school district's website.

If your children are struggling with an assignment, consider immediately simplifying the task by breaking it up into manageable chunks that make it easier to accomplish. Attempting to push through when they are not coping might cause more anxiety, frustration, and anger. I am not saying that the assignment should be left undone, but perhaps taking a breather every so often could make it a more pleasurable experience (notice how I used positive language there!).

Based on my own personal experiences with my daughter *and* students in my classrooms, and supported by a study conducted by Idit Katz, Tamara Buzukashvili, and Liat Feingold of Ben-Gurion University, frustration and anxiety are two reasons why many children don't want to do homework. Moreover, when homework doesn't get finished, children don't want to go to school for fear of getting into trouble. It's a vicious cycle.

The important takeaway here is that if your children are struggling *that* much with homework, you need to reach out to the teacher(s). They (I hope) should be able to make suggestions and guide you to meet the specific needs of your children. Again: The teacher(s) should always be your first contact. They know your children's

ROUTINE VERSUS FLEXIBLE SCHEDULE

current academic levels and should be able to guide you in your quest for dramaless homework.

In the meantime, here are six suggestions for helping you and your family survive homework hell.

1. Set aside a specific time and place for homework, and make sure that it is a consistent part of the daily routine. This gives your children a sense of structure and predictability around homework.

2. Help your children break down bigger assignments into smaller, more manageable pieces. If they can do one small thing at a time, they will feel more in control and have a sense of accomplishment as each portion is finished.

3. Create a quiet and distraction-free place for homework—no TV, no phone, computer only if they need it for the assignment.

4. Encourage your children to take breaks, especially if they're feeling overwhelmed. Set a timer for fifteen to twenty minutes of work time and then five minutes for a break. Then build up the work time (slowly add a minute or two to the timer for work time). While incorporating breaks will increase the total amount of time it takes to get homework finished, it can decrease the pent-up stress and anxiety.

5. Motivate your children with incentives for completed homework. This could be something as simple as a little extra screen time or a special treat.

6. Let your children know that you are there to support and guide them when they need you. Encourage them to work

through challenges on their own, but be available if they need your help. However, do not hover! Don't stand over them and watch every little thing they do! That is not truly helping them become independent. Rather, be present. For example, if your children work at the dining table, stay in the kitchen and prepare dinner, and make eye contact to check in with them. That's being present! (The only things that should hover are helicopters and hummingbirds!)

Keep in mind that every child is unique and that not all approaches will work for all children. You may find that you have to experiment with different strategies to find out what works best for your children and your family.

REAL Important Takeaways

Resilience

Both flexible scheduling and routine can help by providing a sense of predictability and structure as well as allowing for adaptability and creativity depending upon the ever-changing circumstances. When things don't go according to plan, children learn to bounce back and get creative in coming up with solutions and learning to anticipate change.

Empowerment

Routine is empowering because it allows children to establish healthy habits, while flexible scheduling empowers them by giving them more control over time and activities and encouraging creativity.

ROUTINE VERSUS FLEXIBLE SCHEDULE

Autonomy

Routine fosters autonomy by establishing clear expectations and boundaries around activities, allowing individuals and families to plan and prioritize these activities. Flexible scheduling, in turn, allows individuals and families to make choices and decisions about how they will spend their time and which activities they are going to prioritize.

Quality of Family Life

Both routine and flexible scheduling contribute to the quality of family life by providing stability and predictability, which are beneficial for everyone (especially for those with very busy schedules!) and, at the same time, providing opportunities for exploration and creativity. Both can help to create a positive and calm family environment.

The next chapter is about expectations—what they are, why they're important, and who needs them.

But, before you get to expectations, go ahead and think about your schedules, your *must-dos*, and your *want-to-dos*. It's good stuff!

Following, you will find an example of the next activity in your Working Journal at untamedchaosbook.com/resources.

Working Journal Activity 6: Must-Do and Want-to-Do Lists

It's time for you to create your *must-dos* and your *want-to-dos*!

List 1 is the *must-do* list. These are tasks that you have to get done during the day. For example, I have to feed and let out my dog, GusGus. I have to do my "Power Hour" of work time. I have to go to the meeting that is scheduled. I have to go to my doctor's appointment.

List 2 is the *want-to-do* list. These are nonessential activities but ones I would like to do during the day, such as working on a puzzle, reading a novel, or playing in the garden.

Your children's day also should be interspersed with *must-dos* and *want-to-dos*. How? Give them … wait for it … control of their *want-to-do* activity once they have completed their *must-do* activities, or withhold their *want-to-do* activity if they didn't finish their *must-dos*. Let's break it down.

When I was teaching, I used the statement, "If you do _____, then you can do _____." This was my way of getting the *must-dos* done and giving the children control all at the same time. Here's the catch: The children cannot pick their *want-to-do* activities willy-nilly. That is a recipe for disaster, so help them to create their *want-to-do* list carefully.

Let me give you an example.

ROUTINE VERSUS FLEXIBLE SCHEDULE

Must Do	Want to Do
Feed dog	Play video games
Brush teeth	Play ball
Get dressed	Read my book
Eat breakfast	Watch TV
Pack lunch	Color/paint/other craft
Go to school	Play outside
Do homework	Go for a run

On the lines that follow, start a *must-do* and a *want-to-do* list for each person in the family. You might find that you and the children have some of the same *must-dos* on your lists!

UNTAMED CHAOS

Must-Do List

Want-to-Do List

CHAPTER 7

What to Expect With Expectations

"You must take personal responsibility. You cannot change the circumstances, the seasons, or the wind, but you can change yourself."
—Jim Rohn

It's time to dive deeper into expectations. Why? Well ... Because how are you going to know what to expect if you don't have clear expectations?

Discovering your expectations begins by asking yourself a question. In fact, you should ask yourself several questions:

- What do you expect from yourself and from your children?
- How do you expect yourself and your partner to behave in front of your children?
- How do you expect your children to behave?
- What do you want your children to do, for example, when they get home from school or when you have guests in your home?
- How do you want them to treat you and other people?

If you have no ideas, then how can your family, friends, teachers, and children understand what you expect? They can't!

First, you have to understand what expectations really are. Expectations are not simply demands. Nor are they the same as rules. Expectations are assumptions about what should or will happen in certain instances. Expectations are based on past experiences, cultural norms, personal values, and assumptions. They can be implicit, meaning they are implied, or explicit, meaning they are explained and clear. Rules, on the other hand, are typically more formal. They are directives: "Sit down in your seat, go to bed, feed the dog." Rules are more rigid and objective than expectations.

During my time as a positive behavior facilitator, I learned that if I had three to five positive behavior expectations (not rules) both at home and in my classrooms, I could help my children understand their boundaries, take responsibility for their behaviors, and give them freedom to make choices while simultaneously learning from their consequences. Allowing children to have a voice in creating those expectations fosters success in the home, in school, and in their personal lives.

Winner, winner, chicken dinner! Having had success not only in my own home but with my private clients and with students from pre-K through to college, I propose setting explicit expectations for all members of the family.

Expectations for the Entire Family

Hear ye, hear ye, it's time for a town meeting. The purpose of this meeting is to create positive behavior expectations to which every family member will adhere. I know you're thinking, "You're out of your bleeping mind, Dr. Teri." I promise you I'm not! These

WHAT TO EXPECT WITH EXPECTATIONS

tools work. Together with all other family members, you need to create expectations for everyone's specific needs and values, and then communicate them clearly through regular reminders and positive reinforcements. Once you've done this, you've hit gold!

Let's start with an example of family expectations (you can find more examples at untamedchaosbook.com/resources). Remember, everyone has a voice in establishing these!

1. Kindness and respect: Encourage kindness and respect toward family members, friends, and visitors. This includes using polite language and listening to others with an open mind. Avoid name calling or hurtful comments.

2. Responsibility: Encourage each family member to take responsibility for their belongings and to help out with household chores. This includes cleaning up after themselves, making their beds, putting the dishes away, and completing homework and other tasks without being asked more than once.

3. Honesty: Encourage family members (grown-ups included) to be honest with one another and to admit their mistakes. No one is perfect! Learning to say "sorry" is invaluable when trying to create a peaceful home.

4. Safety: Encourage all members of the family to be mindful of safety rules, such as wearing a helmet when riding their bicycle, walking on the sidewalk, and locking the door when everyone leaves.

5. Empathy: Encourage all family members to develop concern for other people. Be sensitive to other people's feelings, offer help when needed, and think about how words and actions might affect someone else.

Expectations for You and Your Spouse

Sometimes you expect certain actions/behavior from your partner, but they didn't get the memo. And sometimes your expectations are simply unrealistic.

It's important to remember that expectations should be realistic, reasonable, and based on mutual agreement and understanding. Obviously, communication is key, and having an open and honest conversation about expectations can ensure that both you and your partner are on the same page and working toward the same outcome. Showing up as a united front is crucial. Here are five steps that you and your partner can take to create a united front.

1. As hard as it may be sometimes, shared responsibility, meaning both parents take responsibility for the care of the home and of the children, reigns supreme when trying to create a peaceful home. This means sharing household chores and child care responsibilities and being supportive of each other.

2. Talk is cheap, so communication should be frequent, open, and honest. Both of you should feel comfortable honestly sharing your needs, concerns, and schedules. You need to be willing to listen to each other's perspectives, and find ways to be supportive of each other's goals.

3. Be flexible and adaptable. Be willing to step up when your partner is overwhelmed, overtired, sick, or just needs a little extra support. Adjust your schedule or change your plans to accommodate the needs of your family.

4. R-E-S-P-E-C-T: Need I say more?

5. T stands for teamwork, and teamwork is key to achieving goals and creating peace and harmony in your home environment. You have to be willing to collaborate on decisions and stand up together when dealing with challenges and conflicts.

Now that you have your team, it's time to get down to the business of creating those expectations and consequences.

Creating Expectations and Consequences

Creating expectations and the consequences of those expectations is an empowering project for everyone involved. You have to allow your children to have a voice and to feel comfortable and confident enough to share their thoughts. If they feel they will be punished in some way for being honest, they will not contribute their thoughts and feelings and may have trouble expressing their needs as they grow older. Use the family expectations examples from earlier to kick-start your own list. But, importantly, make sure that your expectations are just that: yours. Also be sure that the consequences fit the infraction. Being too lenient with consequences can be as bad as being too harsh. Consequences are the best teaching/learning tool out there; make them beneficial, *not* overly punitive!

I know it may sound corny, but holding this town meeting to discuss why it is important to have expectations and consequences is necessary for a healthy family system. Plus, it's empowering to all the members in the system. It gives everyone a chance to share their thoughts and opinions, which allows everyone to be on the same page, use the same words, and promote the same positive behaviors.

1. Identify key behaviors that are important to your family. Use the previous examples to get started.

2. Define the expectation. For example, if being respectful to others is a key behavior, consider defining that expectation as speaking kindly to each other, using manners, listening when others talk, and not interrupting when someone else is speaking.

3. Establish the consequences if the expectation is not met. Here is where many families kind of lose it. You need to make sure that the consequences are fair and proportionate to the behavior. For example, if one of your children is rude, the consequence could be that they have to apologize. An unfair consequence would be sending them to their room without dinner.

4. Once you've identified all the behaviors and the expectations and established the consequences, create a written contract, like the expectation matrix at the end of this chapter. Everyone in the family gets to sign the contract. This way everyone knows and has made a commitment to the expectations that you as a family have created.

Keep in mind that expectations can and probably should be adjusted over time. By encouraging open communication and feedback from each member of the family, you're continuously improving your behavior system!

Holy guacamole, that's a lot of information! But this is a process. All that's required of you is progress with small steps. Don't try to win the race overnight! Creating long-lasting change from untamed chaos into peace and tranquility is going to take time. You cannot rush this. Baby steps grow into bigger steps, and, pretty soon, you'll be marching along like the leader of the parade!

WHAT TO EXPECT WITH EXPECTATIONS

REAL Important Takeaways

Resilience

Realistic expectations can help your family manage storms and setbacks as you all are better able to handle the challenges and more confident in your abilities and the outcomes of your decisions. Unrealistic expectations lead to disappointment, feelings of failure, and a tendency to not want to try new things in the future. The same can be said for consequences. Anticipated/known consequences (positive, negative, or neutral) can reinforce everyone's ability to manage challenges. Unexpected, disproportionate, or unfair consequences can undermine their resilience.

Empowerment

When there are expectations that are clear and realistic, everyone feels more empowered. At the same time, unrealistic or unclear expectations cause confusion and a sense of powerlessness. Here again, known consequences foster your family members' sense of empowerment because they can aim to be rewarded for their efforts and their successes, which helps them feel capable and confident, while unfair consequences take away their sense of control and cause children, in particular, to attach their worth to their actions.

Autonomy

When expectations are clear and realistic, you and your family are more likely to feel that you have control over your lives. On the other hand, unrealistic or unclear expectations lead to feeling helpless and out of control, which, in turn, causes dependency on others. If one individual doesn't believe they're capable of making good decisions, they may rely on others to make decisions for them, which hampers autonomy. Known consequences reinforce everyone's sense of autonomy while unexpected consequences can make them feel like they are being punished.

Quality of Family Life

With clear and realistic expectations, you and your family will feel like you're working toward common goals and that your efforts and contributions are valued by each other. Unrealistic expectations are unclear and lead to conflict, anger, frustration, and dissatisfaction. Likewise, anticipated consequences tend to reinforce positive behaviors and attitudes while discouraging negative ones, which, together, naturally increase the quality of family life. Unexpected, disproportionate, and unfair consequences, however, cause stress and tension.

The next chapter covers boundaries—and I'm not talking about fences! You'll learn to recognize and build your own boundaries to handle those people who will try to put cracks in your wall, a chink in your armor, or doubt, fear, and frustration into your mind.

Before moving on, I want to introduce you to an exercise (which you can find at untamedchaosbook.com/resources) that will kick-start your expectations and consequences town meeting: the expectation matrix.

Working Journal Activity 7: Expectation Matrix

Following is an expectation matrix. Together, you and your family will fill in the expectation (behavior), the definition (what the behavior looks and sounds like), the consequences that happen when the expectation is met, the consequences that happen when it is not met, and special celebrations. Then everyone initials to show their agreement!

UNTAMED CHAOS

Expectation/behavior	Definition	Consequences when met	Consequences when not met	Celebrations	Participants' initials

CHAPTER 8

Surround Yourself With Boundaries

"The best revenge is massive success."
—Frank Sinatra

Have you heard any of the following before?

- You are absolutely crazy.
- You are a bad parent.
- You should put your child on medication.
- Your child is out of control!
- You should've, would've, could've …

I've personally heard it all. And how to deal with these "opinions" is always a hot topic when I speak with private clients and at parenting groups. Lots of people have lots of things to say, and lots of times, it's not helpful (most of the time, it's just downright mean). What do you do to handle these unhelpful comments? Set boundaries.

A "boundary," according to the *Merriam-Webster Dictionary*, is "something that indicates or fixes a limit or extent."

Boundaries are a necessary part of life. They are imperative to your survival. Boundaries are not meant to isolate you; they are meant to protect you. Think of a fence around a yard. Not only does it keep the dog in, it keeps the stray cats out. Boundaries keep what is inside the fence—you and your family—safe physically, emotionally, and mentally.

It is imperative to establish personal and familial boundaries. Personal boundaries are set by and for each individual. Familial boundaries are set by family members with and for each other.

Here's what I mean by personal boundaries:

- Protecting your personal space and privacy.
- Setting limits on how much time you spend with certain people.
- Saying "no" when you don't want to do something.
- Not allowing others to treat you disrespectfully.

Here's what I mean by familial boundaries:

- Establishing specific expectations for behavior.
- Limiting the amount of time spent with or the influence of extended family members.
- Respecting each other's emotional and physical boundaries.
- Protecting each person's privacy and personal space.

Without boundaries, you might feel obligated to respond to everyone else's wants and needs and prioritize them over your own, which can leave you feeling resentful not only toward others but toward yourself. This is detrimental to your individual and familial self-respect.

You need boundaries to protect your privacy and space and to keep your emotional well-being in check. Boundaries provide time and space—for you! For your self-care, sleep, exercise, etc. Time, space, and *people* all influence how you create and maintain your boundaries.

Positive Peeps

Let's talk about who you want in *your* world! I suspect that you want positive people to surround you and your family. (I know I do!)

The Positive Peeps are those people you want to let in and hang out and spend time with. But here too you need to have boundaries. When you are with these people, do you feel respected and valued? Do you feel safe physically and emotionally? Are you calm? Do you trust them, and do they trust you? Do you feel safe expressing your thoughts and opinions? If you answered "yes," those are your Positive Peeps.

Of course, everyone can't be positive all the time. That would be unrealistic. But you want to have positive people around you who can serve as role models for your children. You want to surround yourself and your family with people who help to create a sense of community and belonging. And you definitely want to surround yourself with people who can provide opportunities for growth and development. Such positive people provide the chance to have new experiences, see and hear new ideas, and create a sense of belonging and fulfillment. The best thing about Positive Peeps is that they can and will support you when you're struggling to cope. They provide emotional support and encouragement when you and your family go through difficult times (which you will). When your children see positive behaviors and attitudes being modeled by their parents as well as other positive people, they're more likely to imitate those behaviors.

Negative Nellies

But not all of the people around you are Positive Peeps. The Negative Nellies try to finagle their way in too … and they always have something to say. You want to spend as little time as possible with them. All too often, the Negative Nellies are the people you assume would be the most supportive, like extended family relatives. In fact, they can be the worst kind of Negative Nellies. I know this from my own experiences!

Handling the Negative Nellies can be challenging, especially when they are relatives, but these people will drain all of your energy and resources if you allow them to. It may not be intentional, but they say or do things that have a consistent negative impact on you and your family.

I want to share a quick story to demonstrate that even though challenging the Negative Nellies who *are* your relatives is difficult, it is necessary, and it can be done.

At one point, my husband and I were trying to get our son stable at school. Keep in mind that there had been repeated suspensions, major infractions, tears, fighting, and meetings out the wazoo. One of our family members disagreed with our decision to find a better placement for him at an alternative school. Basically, she told us the reason he was having so many problems was because we didn't know how to parent; that we were doing everything wrong; that anyone would be better parents than us; and that we weren't trying hard enough. Not only did she say those things, she said them at the dinner table in a crowd of fifteen people (our son included). Everyone stared at us, and not one person stood up for us or disagreed with her. We were stunned into silence. After dinner, we left to go home, both of the kids in the back seat. Our son was smug, and our daughter was tearful and silent. We were still shocked and hurt. We began to doubt ourselves even more.

Of course, never had any of those relatives at any point let our son stay with them for a weekend, or take him to the movies, or thought to give us time alone to figure any of this out. Instead, they talked behind our backs, degraded us *to* our son, and enabled him to continue his poor decision making by bashing us at every opportunity.

The initial shock and hurt were followed first by anger and then by sadness. We knew what we had to do to keep from totally falling apart. Those negative feelings turned into resilience and empowerment. We sat down and put into action some very strong boundaries, which I will share now with you. I want you to know that you can, should, and are *capable* of putting boundaries in place too.

What You Can Do With the Negative Nellies

How do you deal with the Negative Nellies? Boundaries! It isn't easy, but when you have clearly identified your individual and family expectations, you have to share them with your Negative Nellies. In order for your boundaries to be honored, or even considered, you have to be explicit! They won't like it. They may act out toward you. They may even try to blame you for their bad behavior. But you can and should verbalize your boundaries and the consequences of crossing those boundaries. With those family members who gave us a really (*really*) difficult time, we stopped going to their house, and we stopped inviting them to ours. We didn't want the energy-draining negativity that they brought with them. No thank you ... No bueno ... Don't let the door hit you on the way out! It was hard! They subversively kept in contact with our son and tried to talk with our daughter (even at a young age, she shut them down and cut off contact). All the while, they blamed us, spoke negatively about us, and enabled our son to continue with his poor choices and his bad behaviors. They undermined whatever consequences we put into effect by making excuses for him ("Boys will be boys" was most common).

As hard as it was, we stuck to our decision, and today, we are much better off because of it.

It's okay to distance yourself and your family from negative people even if they are relatives, especially if they have a negative impact on your life. You have every right to prioritize your well-being and surround yourself with positive people who support you and your family and raise you up.

Define Your Boundaries

Now it's time for you to clarify *your* boundaries. Don't be rash about it, but also don't overthink it. This is for you, your partner, and your children. What is going to be best for all of you?

Here are four steps to help you to create your boundaries.

1. Identify your needs. Reflect on what is important to you and what you need to feel safe, respected, and comfortable. This could include physical boundaries like personal space, emotional boundaries like sharing personal information and managing expectations, and time boundaries like setting limits on how much time you spend with others or how much work you will take on.

2. Communicate your boundaries clearly. Once you figure out your needs, communicate them assertively and clearly to

other people. Using "I" statements rather than blaming or accusing language is a great way to express your needs. For example, use "I need some alone time to recharge" rather than "You are always in my space."

3. Once you establish your boundaries and communicate them clearly, stand your ground and enforce the consequences of overstepped boundaries consistently. It's okay to say "no" when you feel the need to. Stand up for yourself when others try to push your boundaries, and take steps to protect your boundaries if someone tries to break them down. For example, you want to spend some quiet time with your children and/or your partner, but you've been invited to dinner with friends. Saying "no thanks" and telling your friends that you'll take a rain check is *perfectly* acceptable. For another example, say someone wants to come and stay for a week at your home. Telling them that you would like to have them over for dinner but they cannot stay at your house is also *perfectly* acceptable … Perhaps you can suggest some reasonable accommodations not too far from you.

4. Finally, practice self-care to prioritize your own well-being. Take a break when you need one. Engage in activities that bring you joy. And seek support from others when you need it. By taking care of yourself, you can build the strength you need to maintain healthy boundaries in the long run.

REAL Important Takeaways

Resilience

By creating a sense of safety and security, boundaries help families build resilience.

Empowerment

When individuals are permitted to set boundaries about what they will and won't tolerate, they're able to communicate their needs effectively, which gives them a sense of agency and control over their lives.

Autonomy

When individuals and families have clear boundaries around what is and isn't acceptable in their homes and in their individual lives, they are able to exercise their autonomy with their individual values and goals. They can take action independently and make decisions on their own.

Quality of Family Life

When families are able to set boundaries, they're more likely to experience positive relationships and have a greater sense of harmony and closeness within the family system.

When you have clear and healthy boundaries, you have better relationships with the people who are most important and supportive and who have a positive impact on your life.

Boundaries are key to enabling self-care, the topic of the next chapter. I'm going to look at self-care from three different perspectives: alone time, couple time, and family time. But before you get there, take a look at the following boundaries activity (untamedchaosbook.com/resources).

Working Journal Activity 8: Boundaries

Boundaries exist to keep you safe. They are necessary for you to build your self-respect. Without boundaries, you often respond to everyone else's wants and needs and neglect your own. Considering all of this, who do you and who don't you want in your life?

First, create a list of the Positive Peeps you enjoy spending time with and want to keep in your life. This can be a lot of fun.

Next, create a list of the Negative Nellies—those people who drain your energy; who aren't respectful toward you or your time; who expect you to stop what you're doing because they "need" to see or talk to you; and who won't respond kindly when you say "no" to them or put them off.

Who on that list can you kindly eliminate? Who on that list has to be in your life in some capacity?

Think about some ways that you can respond to the Negative Nellies that you must live with. For example, your sister doesn't like your boyfriend and makes no bones about telling you every blessed time she talks to you. You may respond by saying, "Thanks for the input, but we are going to have to agree to disagree." Or as soon as she starts, say something like, "I really don't want to have this discussion again. We can either end our call or move onto another topic." You do *not* have to stay engaged with the Negative Nellies. You have plenty of other positive and productive things to do in your life!

Now ... It's time to refine your boundaries. Complete the following sentences, included here as examples, in your Working Journal (at untamedchaosbook.com/resources) to refine your boundaries.

a. I am worthy of

_____

b. It bothers me when people

_____

c. My physical boundaries are

_____

d. My emotional boundaries are

_____

e. When I feel my boundaries are crossed, I will

_____

f. I value my time and energy by

_____

g. I will take time for self-care by

_____

It is almost impossible to not spend some time with people who are negative, but by creating boundaries, you can protect and value yourself, your time, and your worth.

CHAPTER 9

Self-Care Is Not Selfish

"The more joy we shared, the more joy we had. And the more joy we had, the more joy we could share."
—His Holiness the Dalai Lama and Archbishop Desmond Tutu, The Little Book of Joy

"I don't have time for yoga."

"It is selfish of me to go to dance class when my children have homework."

"I'm going to get the children and the dry cleaning, and after I cook dinner and clean up, I'll do something for myself … if I have time."

Sound familiar? Does making time for yourself seem impossible? Do you feel like even if you could, you're selfish to put yourself first?

Self-care is absolutely not selfish! In fact, a lack of self-care can result in burnout—exhaustion, anger, and frustration, as well as preventable physical and mental health challenges. And then you definitely can't show up as your best self. Self-care is a vital part of your overall well-being. Here's the rub: It takes intentional and deliberate actions to take care of yourself.

Likewise, it takes that same intention and deliberate action for a family to take care of itself. Family self-care is vital to its health and well-being. Remember, families are systems—if one cog in the system isn't working the way it should, the whole system is affected. While it's often associated with personal alone time (and that's an important facet), self-care also applies to couple alone time and family alone time. I often get asked, "How can it be alone time if it is with the children or my partner?" Excellent question! In your quest for tranquility, you aren't traveling alone. The people around you add value to your life, and in the same way, you add value to theirs. Relationships require nurturing, and if you don't prioritize them, you will take them for granted and compromise them. This is why alone time is vital to you, your partner, and your family.

In the next section, I'm going to break down self-care into alone, couple, and family self-care and include suggestions on nutrition, physical health, spiritual wellness, and emotional health for each.

Nutrition is a critical component of self-care because it directly impacts your physical and mental health. When you have a balanced diet, you get the nutrients you need to maintain energy levels and support your immune system. In contrast, eating unhealthy foods, such as fats, processed foods, and sugar, can lead to serious health issues including heart disease, diabetes, and obesity. I am not saying that these foods should never be part of your diet. I love fried calamari, pizza, and ice cream (not together, mind you). But if you eat these foods in moderation and recognize why it's important to prioritize nutrition as part of your self-care routine, you can enjoy being healthier all together.

Physical health is an important aspect of self-care. Regular physical activity strengthens your systems and helps to regulate your body weight. Physical activity has been shown to have a positive effect on mental well-being too as exercise triggers endorphins that promote feelings of happiness and reduce anxiety and stress. Exercise also provides time for reflection. While exercising, you can organize your thoughts, gain perspective, and just plain clear your mind. Find an activity that you enjoy and that meets your goals for self-care. Healthcare professionals are often the best folks to guide you to a suitable new routine.

Spirituality is also important to self-care because it goes beyond the physical and mental aspects. It addresses the inner depths of well-being. Spirituality encompasses being self-reflective and self-aware. It gives you the opportunity to explore your own values and beliefs. Reflecting on your inner thoughts and feelings can lead to a deeper understanding of yourself. Recognize that spirituality is very personal and individual. There's no right or wrong because it's yours. But don't force what is yours onto someone else. They are on their own journey.

Emotional health is a weather forecast of your overall well-being and how you navigate through life. It is important to acknowledge your emotions and try to understand *why* you feel what you feel. Managing your emotions also is important to taking care of yourself. After all, emotions influence your self-awareness, how you handle stress, what happens in your relationships, how you treat yourself, and how you treat others. Being emotionally aware and understanding how to regulate your emotions might include activities like journaling, mindfulness, therapy, or counseling. It's important to remember that every person's journey is just that: their unique, one-of-a-kind journey. What works best for one person is not necessarily what works best for someone else.

Me, Myself, and I Care

- Nutrition: Treat yourself by preparing and enjoying a healthy nourishing meal. Take that alone time to try out new recipes or maybe even enjoy your meal in silence without any distractions.

- Physical: This is the time to prioritize exercise. You might practice yoga, do strength training, or go on a bike ride or a nice long walk. However you choose to spend this time, fill it with something that fills your cup.

- Spiritual: Perhaps you spend your time in meditation or reflection, maybe even prayer. This is your time—define what is important to you.

- Emotional: During this time, you might journal, practice gratitude, listen to music, read a book, work in the garden, or even go to therapy. Check in with your emotions, assess what you need, and nurture yourself.

I know there are times when you are so busy that you think, "How am I ever going to find time for myself?" Even if you can only manage ten minutes alone on the bathroom floor or in a chair in the backyard, take it. You need to take "me time."

Keeping the Honeymoon Alive

Despite what many people may say, the honeymoon isn't over! Couple alone time is important for many reasons. It is an opportunity to raise each other up, especially when one of you is feeling down.

- Nutrition: Use your couple time to plan out and prepare a nice meal for the two of you so that you can enjoy it together without interruptions. Preparing the meal together allows you both to slow down and connect.

- Physical: Get those endorphins flowing! Maybe take a dance class together, go for a long walk, or even do yoga. Or just take a nap together!

- Spiritual: You might meditate together or simply have a quiet conversation. Perhaps attend a religious service if that is meaningful to both of you.

- Emotional: Use this time to check in with each other, have deep conversations, or discuss something that is bothering you (without blaming—remember to use "I" statements to express your needs). Practice gratitude for one another, and if necessary, choose to attend couples therapy together.

One of my favorite times of the week is date night. Just me and Dr. Fred. Sometimes, we binge on Netflix; sometimes, we go to the movie theater or a local pizza joint. Other times, we just sit in our rocking chairs (yes, we do have matching rocking chairs!) and look out the back window. But this is us. You can determine what works for you as a couple.

Your Monkeys, Your Circus

Time to spend some family alone time! No extended family! No friends! Just you and your circus!

- Nutrition: Plan a healthy meal, go shopping for the ingredients, and have everybody help in the meal preparation. It's a great way to spend time teaching and learning with your children.

- Physical: This is a great way to bond with your children and create lasting memories. Take walks or go on hikes; play outdoor games; do a family fitness challenge. Maybe just jump into the pool together!

- Spiritual: For some families, attending a religious service together might be valuable. For others, meditating and sitting quietly may be worth trying.

- Emotional: This is the time to have family discussions or simply spend time together without distractions (which means putting work away and focusing on your family). It might include a game night or putting a puzzle together.

Whatever you do, make it special. It doesn't have to be fancy; ice cream and a movie, a trip to the mall, a candlelit picnic on the family room floor—celebrate yourselves and each other. Be creative!

These three levels of self-care—individual, couple, and family—will help you move from untamed chaos into peace and tranquility. They are real opportunities to connect with yourself, your partner, and your children on a variety of levels. Understand that everything isn't going to change overnight. You have to do the work, but these are ways to get yourself started on that path.

REAL Important Takeaways

Resilience

Practicing self-care provides resources necessary to manage stress, regulate emotions, and maintain a positive outlook on life. With these tools, everyone is better able to handle challenges and setbacks.

Empowerment

Self-care enhances empowerment when families prioritize their needs and desires. You are deliberately taking action to support your physical, emotional, and spiritual well-being.

Autonomy

Practicing self-care autonomously encourages each family member to prioritize their own needs and choices that support their own individual well-being. Each member is responsible for their own self-care.

Quality of Family Life

When family members take care of themselves, they are better able to take care of others who might need them.

Prioritizing self-care means that families are better equipped to cope with challenges; they feel more in control; and the home becomes a more supportive and healthy family environment.

In the next chapter, I'm going to share how you can reach out to me personally. Remember, you shouldn't be on this journey alone. But before you get there, take a look at the following Self-Care Checklist, which is available in the Working Journal at untamedchaosbook.com/resources.

Working Journal Activity 9: Self-Care Checklist

This is an example of a Self-Care Checklist. Self-care is a personal journey, so you will need to customize this checklist to fit your own unique needs.

Nutrition

By prioritizing nutrition as part of your self-care routine, you can enjoy more energy and vitality, support your overall health and well-being, and become more resilient in the process.

- Eat balanced meals.
  - Fruits
  - Veggies
  - Whole grains
  - Lean proteins
  - Healthy fats
- Drink plenty of water.
- Limit sugar.
- Be mindful of what and when you eat.

Being conscious about what you eat, the quality and the quantity, ensures that you get the nutrition that your body and mind need to remain healthy and to maintain a healthy weight. In addition, you are modeling for your children how to make good choices, how to keep yourself healthy, and why nutrition is so important.

Physical Health

By incorporating more physical activity into your self-care routine, you can boost your mood, increase your vitality and energy, and improve your overall well-being and health.

- Participate in regular physical activity, like walking, running, biking, and swimming.
- Stretch or practice yoga.
- Establish sleep hygiene.
- Take breaks throughout the day to move and stretch.

Taking time each day to move is important because it helps to support your physical health, maintain good posture, reduce stress and anxiety, and benefit your overall well-being.

Spiritual Wellness

When you incorporate spiritual well-being as a part of your self-care routine, you can handle stress and navigate challenges more effectively. Spirituality helps when coping with difficult emotions, and it can bring focus to a more purpose-driven life.

- Practice meditation, prayer, or journaling.
- Spend time in nature; take a walk.
- Practice gratitude, and focus on the positive things in your life.
- Do something that brings you a sense of purpose.

Emotional Health

Incorporating emotional health as part of your self-care program cultivates a greater sense of calm and inner peace as well as develops a greater sense of self-awareness.

- Be kind to yourself, give yourself grace. Speak affirmations over yourself.
- Connect with loved ones, and encourage supportive relationships.
- Do what brings you joy and makes you feel happy.
- Seek help (professional if necessary) if you're struggling with depression or anxiety.

CHAPTER 10

Pearls and Diamonds

"Start by doing what's necessary; then do what's possible; and suddenly you are doing the impossible."
—St. Francis of Assisi

Holy smokes! Have you crossed the finish line? Parenting is a lifelong marathon. Some miles are easier than others, but, overall, it is not easy. Nothing worth working for ever is.

For this marathon, there is no finish line. Once a parent, always a parent. It's a lifelong appointment. There is no quitting or retiring. Your children will always be your children (even the ones who choose to separate from you).

I want you to know that I am here to be of service to you! You can always reach out to me at drterirouse.com. You can schedule a call, access the resources page, and subscribe to the *Snuggle Bunny Book Club*™ all in one place.

With all of this new-found knowledge, your wonderful, exciting, love-filled, peaceful, and tranquil journey is about to begin. The world is your oyster, and you are creating pearls ... diamonds even. The most beautiful things start out as a grain of sand or a dingy rock. Over time, in a shell surrounded by slime and grime, or deep in the ground under immense and constant pressure, they become beautiful. They become precious. The same can be said of you and your family.

You may have felt stuck in the slime or under pressure, but now you can navigate through that. You have the tools, you have the strategies, you have the skills. You even have a Working Journal and a compilation of all of the "REAL Important Takeaways." You've got this!

My fellow parents, you are all perfectly imperfect! You do the best that you can with who you are, where you are, and what you know. And now you know more. That is one of the reasons why I wrote this book. It's the reason that I so passionately want you to embrace your family—not only physically but emotionally.

Just as important as going to school and work, just as important as eating and sleeping, just as important as working hard, is playing and loving hard. In the back of this book are several resources. I have included a couple of my favorite positive behavior intervention websites as well as links to useful articles. These resources are meant to help you find the balance of working hard and playing hard together. Some of the suggestions won't be for you and your family, and that's okay! They are ideas to spark your creativity.

My website also includes several bonuses, like fun activities for you and your family, a list of virtual field trips, and books that I find enjoyable and helpful.

Now go forth, celebrate, work hard, play hard, love hard, and share the joy. And remember: You're doing the best you can, and you are worth it!

A Note from Me to You

As we end this chapter of your journey to peace and tranquility, my most profound wish is for you to know that all things are possible. That you have the power to implement the tools and strategies I've shared with you in this book. Taking one step at a time leads you down the path to the life that you and your family yearn for and that you are worthy of.

The life you want is waiting for you. Doesn't it feel good to know that you have everything you need inside ... just waiting to be unlocked?

You are taking very brave action by stepping into this way of parenting and being.

Remember, chaos is temporary. It's never too late to change direction. And you don't need to do this alone—I am right here with you!

Reach out to me at drterirouse.com if you have any questions about the tools and strategies in this book or if you just want to share your success with me!

Your sister in REAL Peaceful Parenting with grace, peace, and tranquility,

Dr. Teri

About the Author

Dr. Teri Rouse, Ed.D, or Dr. Teri to friends, family, students, and clients, has a mission to empower parents to overcome chaos and restore peace in their homes through a variety of techniques and strategies. Through her own life experiences, a love of learning, and a passion for helping families, she has dedicated her career to making a positive impact on children, parents, and educators.

Working with students and private clients from diverse cultural and socioeconomic backgrounds, she develops and implements customized positive behavior interventions. Taking the best of the best strategies and techniques, she created the REAL Peaceful Parenting framework. She also has a program for young adults called Braver Than You Believe to guide them to overcome fear and worry, gain confidence, and discover their inner strength.

Dr. Teri has spent more than thirty years in classrooms as a special education teacher, behavior and early interventionist, autism specialist, and applied behavior analyst, in addition to founding and serving as the managing director of KIDS:

Interventions & Direct Services. Additionally, for seventeen years, Dr. Teri has taught teachers how to teach at Chestnut Hill College, Widener University, and Penn State.

An educational coach and consultant and international speaker, she travels the globe to give presentations at conferences for teachers, school administrators, organizations, and conventions. She is involved with the Division of International Special Education and Services, the Council for Exceptional Children (CEC), Autism Speaks, Lily's Hope Foundation, and Uthando, a South African nonprofit tourism and community development initiative.

Dr. Teri has authored multiple bestselling books and is a member of the National Academy of Best-Selling Authors® and a recipient of the Quilly® Award for *Success* with Jack Canfield and *Never Give Up* with Dick Vitale. Inspired by decades of working with children, she authored *Julian's Gift*, a picture book that tells the story of one young boy in her class. In addition, Dr. Teri created the *Snuggle Bunny Book Club*™, a subscription service that enables families to bond over hand-picked, engaging books delivered weekly.

She has been featured on ABC, CBS, NBC, FOX News, Bravo, the Success Network, *USA Today*, *Miami Herald*, Boston.com, and more.

For Dr. Teri's tips, tools, techniques, and resources, go to untamedchaosbook.com/resources.

For more information about Dr. Teri and her programs, visit:

drterirouse.com
Facebook: Dr. Teri Rouse
Instagram: dr_teri_rouse

Testimonials

I first met Dr. Teri in August 2010 as a graduate student in her class "Classroom Management for Students with Cognitive Disabilities." While Dr. Teri's main focus was on students with cognitive disabilities, I found that her strategies and relevant applications could apply to any and all home and classroom environments.

I've now begun my eighteenth year as a teacher, and my classroom management is still directly influenced by what I learned from Dr. Teri.

First and foremost, she taught educators to treat all students with respect and kindness. As a parent and an experienced educator, I can confirm that the children who need love the most ask for it in the most unloving way.

Second, Dr. Teri reframed my thinking by saying, "You don't know what a student has gone through before they got to school." I've held fast to that mindset, and it has made a significant impact on the climate of my classroom.

Giovanna Gallagher, M.Ed.
Parent, teacher, special education representative,
Pennsylvania and Indiana

Dr. Teri is wholeheartedly the reason why I am a special education professional today. Being a student in her classroom was a true gift. She is why I teach with a gentle and kind heart and always put the child first. Dr. Teri gave me some of the most valuable tools, resources, and experiences, which helped me develop into the parent and teacher I am today.

The most valuable lesson I learned from Dr. Teri is that every child that sits in my classroom has a challenge that I know absolutely nothing about. It is my job as an educator to teach and love the entire child from the moment they step foot in my classroom. Even the most difficult children deserve love, acceptance, and patience.

I am expecting my first child very soon, and I can already see the personal value in her lessons. Her strategies and techniques put the child first with love, understanding, patience, and positivity.

I can only hope to be half the parent, educator, advocate, and leader she is one day.

Melissa Kennedy
Parent, elementary and special education professional,
Pennsylvania and New Jersey

TESTIMONIALS

As a parent, my desire is to help my children have greater opportunities than I was given. Not just financially, but physically, emotionally, and spiritually. I wanted to help them succeed from the minute I laid eyes on them. However, I found out very quickly that my life would never be the same—stress, chaos, and exhaustion became a staple as in most families' lives.

As a parent to three amazing children who are five and under, I always look for new ways to help support them and calm the chaos that inevitably finds its way into our home. Whether it's fighting about which shoes to wear, or wanting to wear two left feet, or encouraging them to clean up after themselves, the battles of toddlers and teens are not for the faint of heart.

Dr. Teri Rouse not only has the mind, credentials, education, and the personal and professional experience of working with families to bring peace into their home, she has a passion for seeing families thrive. Her strategies for parents and their children (but mostly for parents) are tried and true and a practical approach to calming the chaos in any home.

I first met Dr. Teri in 2015 in a professional capacity. However, it wasn't long before I considered her a friend. She knew me before I had my three children and has watched them grow over the years through social media. Dr. Teri has a big heart and a deep desire to create calm out of the chaos that many of us parents find ourselves in each and every day. Her approach to helping families, while straightforward, is profound, practical, and effective. She's an inspiring colleague, educator, mom, and friend; an advocate for children; and an ambassador of hope for parents around the world.

Zack Viscomi
Parent, president/COO, Celebrity Branding® Agency

Snuggle Bunny Book Club™

If you're looking for a way to give your children the one thing they want most—your positive attention—as well as a way to step back into your own childhood, check out the *Snuggle Bunny Book Club*™ at drterirouse.com/SBBC.

The *Snuggle Bunny Book Club*™ offers an opportunity for families to bond over books and create memories that will last a lifetime with a weekly subscription that includes hand-picked, engaging books accompanied by audiovisual content. The *Snuggle Bunny Book Club*™ provides a fun and educational escape and gives families the chance to cuddle up together and enjoy a good book.

Lily's Hope Foundation

The Lily's Hope Foundation provides emergency support to families who face unexpected and urgent needs due to their baby's premature birth. It supports NICU families through Packages of Hope, care packages that are assembled for each family's specific needs; the Preemie Pantry; Holiday Hope Baskets; and the Lily's Hope Foundation Facebook Family Support Groups. These programs are ever-growing and ever-changing to stay current with the needs of families with premature babies.

Visit lilyshopefoundation.org/donate for all the different ways to donate to the Lily's Hope Foundation.

Resources

Autonomy

Brightwheel. "Autonomy in Child Development." *Child Development Blog*, 07 Apr. 2023, blog.mybrightwheel.com/autonomy-child-development.

Big Emotions

Zhang, Xiaoying, et al. "Influences of Emotion on Driving Decisions at Different Risk Levels: An Eye Movement Study." *Frontiers in Psychology*, vol. 13-2022, 04 Feb. 2022, doi.org/10.3389/fpsyg.2022.788712.

Empowerment

Kitching, Dorothy. "The empowerment of children: Who decides?" *Accident and Emergency Nursing*, vol. 6, no. 1, Jan. 1998, pp. 11–14, doi.org/10.1016/S0965-2302(98)90051-0.

Homework

Katz, Idit, et al. "Homework Stress: Construct Validation of a Measure." *The Journal of Experimental Education*, vol. 80, no. 4, 2012, pp. 405–21, jstor.org/stable/26594362.

Mindless Eating

Wansink, Brian, and Jeffery Sobal. "The 200 Daily Food Decisions

We Overlook." *Environment and Behavior*, vol. 39, no. 1, Jan. 2007, doi.org/10.1177/001391650629557.

Outdoor Fun

365 Atlanta Traveler. "99 Insanely Fun Things to Do Outside (that Are Cheap and Easy)." *365atlantatraveler.com*, 365atlantatraveler.com/fun-things-to-do-outside.

Positive Behavior Supports

Center on Positive Behavioral Interventions and Supports, PBIS.org.

PBIS World, pbisworld.com.

Praise

Corpus, Jennifer Henderlong, and Mark Lepper. "The Effects of Person Versus Performance Praise on Children's Motivation: Gender and age as moderating factors." *Educational Psychology*, vol. 27, no. 4, 25 July 2007, pp. 487–508, doi.org/10.1080/01443410601159852.

Kamins, Melissa, and Carol Dweck. "Person versus process praise and criticism: Implications for contingent self-worth and coping." *Developmental Psychology*, vol. 35, no. 3, 1999, pp. 835–47, doi.org/10.1037/0012-1649.35.3.835.

Quality of Family Life

Brown, Roy, and Ivan Brown. "Family Quality of Life."

RESOURCES

Encyclopedia of Quality of Life and Well-Being Research (A.C. Michalos, ed.), pp. 2194–2201. Springer, Dordrecht, 2014, doi.org/10.1007/978-94-007-0753-5_1006.

Resilience

Mayo Clinic Staff. "Resilience: Build skills to endure hardship." mayoclinic.org, 14 July 2022, mayoclinic.org/tests-procedures/resilience-training/in-depth/resilience/art-20046311.

Writing

Umejima, Keita, et al. "Paper Notebooks vs. Mobile Devices: Brain Activation Differences During Memory Retrieval." *Frontiers in Behavioral Neuroscience*, vol. 15-2021, 19 Mar. 2021, doi.org: 10.3389/fnbeh.2021.634158.

www.ingramcontent.com/pod-product-compliance
Lightning Source LLC
Chambersburg PA
CBHW050727010526
44107CB00009B/769